D1610826

▶ **Seeing Ourselves Through Technology**

DOI: 10.1057/9781137476661.0001

Also by Jill Walker Rettberg

BLOGGING (*2nd edn, 2014*)

DIGITAL CULTURE, PLAY AND IDENTITY: A World of Warcraft Reader
(*edited with H. G. Corneliussen, 2008*)

DOI: 10.1057/9781137476661.0001

palgrave▸pivot

Seeing Ourselves Through Technology: How We Use Selfies, Blogs and Wearable Devices to See and Shape Ourselves

Jill Walker Rettberg
University of Bergen, Norway

palgrave
macmillan

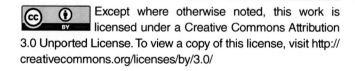
DOI: 10.1057/9781137476661.0001

© Jill Walker Rettberg 2014

The author has asserted her right to be identified as the author of this work in accordance with the Copyright, Designs and Patents Act 1988.

First published 2014 by
PALGRAVE MACMILLAN

Palgrave Macmillan in the UK is an imprint of Macmillan Publishers Limited, registered in England, company number 785998, of Houndmills, Basingstoke, Hampshire, RG21 6XS

Palgrave Macmillan in the US is a division of St Martin's Press LLC, 175 Fifth Avenue, New York, NY 10010.

Palgrave Macmillan is the global academic imprint of the above companies and has companies and representatives throughout the world.

Palgrave® and Macmillan® are registered trademarks in the United States, the United Kingdom, Europe and other countries

ISBN: 978-1-137-47665-4 EPUB
ISBN: 978-1-137-47666-1 PDF
ISBN: 978-1-137-47664-7 Hardback

A catalogue record for this book is available from the British Library.

A catalog record for this book is available from the Library of Congress.

www.palgrave.com/pivot

DOI: 10.1057/9781137476661

Contents

DOI: 10.1057/9781137476661.0001

Acknowledgements

This book was written while I was on sabbatical, and although I have been thinking about the ideas and practices discussed in this book for many years, I would not have been able to write this book without that time to devote to research. My sabbatical was funded by the University of Bergen and by a Leiv Eiriksson fellowship from the Norwegian Research Council that allowed me to spend the first half of 2014 in the United States. I also received generous funding from the University of Bergen's Open Access Publication Fund, which made it possible to publish this under a CC-BY license. I am grateful to work at a university that is willing to try out new models for supporting open access to scholarship. Thank you also to Palgrave Macmillan for experimenting with this model.

My host for my sabbatical in the United States was the Communications Department at the University of Illinois at Chicago (UIC), and I would particularly like to thank Steve Jones and Zizi Papacharissi for generously inviting me to spend a semester there. Steve also gave me opportunities to share my research, and I received very useful feedback from professors and students in the department and in the UIC Digital Humanities Working Group. Thanks as well to the International Office at UIC, and to the Norwegian Research Council's guide for Norwegian scholars going on a scholarly exchange to the United States. I had no idea how many practicalities were needed for an international exchange: the visa, finding an apartment, renting out our own apartment, finding schools and getting all the health paperwork settled for the kids, car insurance and much more. I was glad to have competent guides both at UIC and at home – and it was all very much worth it.

While in the United States, I have had the opportunity to discuss the ideas presented in this book with colleagues at several other universities. Thank you to Nick Montfort for hosting me at MIT for ten days and for very fruitful discussions with colleagues in Cambridge and Boston. I was also invited to present this work at Brown University, at Winona State University and at Wilfred Laurier University, and at all these places I learnt about new things, heard stories or gained new perspectives that I have integrated into the book. Thank you very much to Elli Mylonas, Davin Heckman and Jeremy Hunsinger for arranging these talks. I would also like to thank Lars Nyre and UH-nett Vest for arranging the Medium Design seminar in London in December 2013, where I first presented the general plan of this book.

Writing about digital media I have found a lot of inspirations online. In addition to reading blogs and finding relevant material from links on Twitter and Facebook, I found great support and inspiration in the Selfie Research Network established on Facebook by Terri Senft. It has been very valuable to be able to throw out an idea and get instant feedback, to share bibliographies and case studies, and to find a likeminded community of scholars interested in studying these forms of self-representation online. Many thanks also to Annette Markham for very useful feedback on chapter 3 and to my reviewers for many excellent suggestions.

Thank you to my colleagues in the University of Bergen Electronic Literature Research Group and the Digital Culture Research Group for frequent discussions and day to day support. Thanks also to the University of Bergen library, and especially the research librarian for digital culture, Aud Gjersdal, for exceptional library assistance. And thank you to everyone at The Wormhole Coffee for providing a writing environment where you can sip an excellent coffee with a dragon pattern on top for hours surrounded by other diligently typing people all in a time-travel themed environment.

Most of all, I am grateful to my family. My husband Scott Rettberg has been my trusted colleague and beloved best friend for over a decade, and his input and our discussions always inform my work. My daughter Aurora shows me how to see other parts of the Internet than I usually see. She patiently taught me to understand Tumblr and to chat more visually. I get some of my best leads from links she sends me. My little ones, Jessie and Benji, have taught me that selfies are fascinating to even the youngest among us, and they keep me laughing and climbing and playing. Thank you.

DOI: 10.1057/9781137476661.0002

OPEN

1

Written, Visual and Quantitative Self-Representations

Abstract: *There are three distinct modes of self-representation in digital media: written, visual and quantitative. Each mode has a separate pre-digital history, each of which is presented briefly in this chapter. Blog and written status updates are descendents of diaries, memoirs, commonplace books and autobiographies. Selfies are descendants of visual artists' self-portraits, and the quantitative modes of lifelogs, personal maps, productivity records and activity trackers are descendants of genres such as accounting, habit tracking and to-do lists. In today's digital culture, the three modes are intertwined. Digital self-representation is conversational and allows new voices to be heard. However, society disciplines digital self-representations such as selfies and blogs through ridicule and pathologising.*

Rettberg, Jill Walker. *Seeing Ourselves Through Technology: How We Use Selfies, Blogs and Wearable Devices to See and Shape Ourselves*. Basingstoke: Palgrave Macmillan, 2014. DOI: 10.1057/9781137476661.0003.

In 1524 Parmigianino painted his *Self-Portrait in a Convex Mirror*. Parmigianino used oil paints to paint on the hollow inside of half a wooden ball, to mimic the shape of the mirror he copied his reflection from. The distortions of the convex mirror are exactly replicated in Parmigianino's self-portrait. His hand is in the foreground, grossly distorted by the fish-eye perspective of the convex mirror he is looking into to see himself. We can just see the short pencil he is holding to sketch his own image. We see what he sees.

Parmigianino used a convex mirror to see himself; today we use digital technologies. We snap selfies on our phones and post them to Instagram. We write about our lives in blogs and in status updates to Facebook. We wear activity trackers on our wrists, log our productivity and allow Facebook and other apps to track our locations continuously. The data we track is displayed back to us as graphs, maps, progress charts and timelines. Parmigianino's self-portrait may not seem to have much in common with a FitBit user's charts of steps and sleep patterns, but both are examples of how technology is a means to see part of ourselves. Whether we use a wearable, networked step-counter or a convex mirror and oil paints, technology can reflect back to us a version of who we are. And the data, filters and social media we use to see and share our reflections distort our images in their own particular ways, just as Parmigianino's convex mirror distorted the perspective of his face.

With digital cameras, smart phones and social media it is easier to create and share our self-representations. But self-representations have always been part of our culture. We have drawn, carved, sculpted and painted images of ourselves for millennia; we have kept diaries, scrapbooks and photo albums; we have sung ballads and told stories about ourselves. Sometimes we use the mediation of technology to help us see ourselves better, to understand ourselves or to improve ourselves, or simply to imagine someone to speak to, a 'dear diary' to tell our secrets to when nobody else will listen. Other times we want to share our experiences with others. We paste photos and memorabilia into a photo album to share with family and imagine one day passing it down to our children and their children. Some of us write autobiographies or memoirs to be published for a wider audience.

This book explores the ways in which we represent ourselves today through digital technologies. Like Parmigianino, we create visual self-portraits and share them. Similar to Augustine and Montaigne, who wrote the first autobiography and the first personal essays, we write

DOI: 10.1057/9781137476661.0003

about our thoughts and our experiences. Like Benjamin Franklin and the farmer keeping a weather diary, we track our habits, locations, to-do lists and other data about our lives.

In this book I aim to show how these strands of self-representation intertwine in digital media in three distinct modes: visual, written and quantitative. In the following chapters, I discuss selfies and photographs as tools for self-improvement and self-knowledge and the power relationships that shift and are contested when new groups of people share their self-representations in the public sphere. In chapter 3, I propose using the word 'filter' not just to describe Instagram filters or the filtering of the posts we see in our Facebook newsfeeds but also as an analytical term that allows us to understand how certain aspects of our self-expressions are removed or filtered out, and how our self-expression may be altered as we use different technologies, genres and modes to represent ourselves. Chapter 4 discusses the ways in which wearable tracking devices and web services are automating our self-representations and writing our diaries for us. In chapter 5 I look at our new trust in quantitative data, even to express our experiences and emotions. And finally, in chapter 6, I discuss the balance between self-expression and surveillance. Although we take selfies, post updates to Facebook and use a step-counter, others are putting together the data we generate to create their own representations of us.

But first, let us consider the three key modes of self-representation that this book is about: visual, written and quantitative. There are other possible modes. Curation is one, whether we are showing our identity through our record or book collections or by our careful reblogs or retweets on Tumblr or Twitter, or by sharing the music we listen to on Spotify in playlists or as automated Facebook updates. Music, sounds and dance are other modes for self-representation. But for this study I focus on image, text and numbers.

Self-representation online began in text, with images and some sounds being added as graphical browsers were introduced. The visual turn in social media has been particularly strong in the last few years, especially after smart phones with cameras and fast broadband connections for downloading images and video files became increasingly accessible. The quantitative mode of self-representation has also grown vastly in the last few years as wearable devices have made self-tracking easy with consumer devices and as we in parallel have become aware of the extent to which our data is collected and analysed by commercial companies and by governments.

DOI: 10.1057/9781137476661.0003

Writing about the self

We humans have carved, painted, drawn, sculpted and written about ourselves since we first found ways of making marks in the world. One of the early theorists of the autobiography, Georges Gusdorf (1991), put it thus:

> [T]he very first man who set out to speak and write his name inaugurated a new mode of human presence in the world. Beginning with the very first one, any inscription is an inscription of the self, the signature of an individual who tacks himself onto Nature, thus affording himself room to reflect upon and to transmute its meaning. (qtd by Serfaty 2004)

Augustine's *Confessions*, written in 397–8 CE, is generally recognised as the first autobiography, but writing about oneself was rare until the late sixteenth century. In the Western tradition, diary writing began with spiritual and religious self-examination.

An important reason that people for most of human history only rarely wrote about themselves is the lack of available technology. Paper was expensive, but most importantly, until the last 200 years or so, most people couldn't read and write. In most of Europe, approximately 20–30% of the population were literate in the early seventeenth century, while 70–90% could read and write by the end of the nineteenth century (Chartier 2001, 125). This is likely one reason why early autobiographies, such as Augustine's *Confessions*, were written by priests and nuns, who were more likely than others to have learned to read and write. Almost 1,000 years passed after Augustine's book before autobiographies began to become more common. This may have had to do with social ideas of what was appropriate behaviour as well as to do with literacy and access to pen and paper. In the late sixteenth century, Montaigne noted that drawing yourself was more acceptable than writing about yourself. In one of his many personal essays, he wonders upon seeing the king of Sicily presenting the king of France with a portrait he had drawn of himself, 'why is it not in like manner lawful for everyone to draw himself with a pen, as he did with a crayon?' (Montaigne 1910). His essays, with their digressions and subjective style, were in themselves an important example of the first person becoming prominent in literature.

The first English language autobiography and possibly the first in Europe after Augustine was *The Book of Margery Kempe,* written by Margery Kempe in 1373. Like Augustine's *Confessions,* Kempe's book

DOI: 10.1057/9781137476661.0003

told the story of her spiritual life, though her story is, according to Peter Heehs (2013), 'long and somewhat tedious', mostly dealing with her travels in the Holy Land and Italy (31).

By the late eighteenth century the personal diary had become common. Heehs (2013) describes a move from the accounting ledgers necessary for running a business in the renaissance, where people would often add personal notes to their financial accounts, to the 'scores of English Puritans ... keeping their daily accounts with God on paper manuscripts' by the end of the sixteenth century (8). As paper became cheaper and a wider group of people learned to read and write, personal diaries, not necessarily meant for publication, became increasingly common.

It is important to remember that diaries not intended for publication might have still been shared to a greater degree than the private, padlocked diaries that we often think of today when we imagine personal, non-digital diaries. In her study of early blogging, Vivane Serfaty (2004) compares blogs to the diaries of the Puritans, which were, she writes, 'a requirement of religious self-discipline' that 'recounted a spiritual journey towards personal salvation' (5). In this tradition one examines one's own flaws and failures, seeing self-examination as the source for self-improvement and attaining grace. As we see in later chapters, this is much the same stance as we see in productivity apps and the Quantified Self movement.

Heehs argues that the increased availability of books, increased literacy, and not least the growth of Protestantism and its insistence on each Christian's individual relationship with God led to what he calls a 'radical alteration of the way people looked at themselves and the world.' Heehs continues: 'It became normal for people to examine their own consciences, and many expressed their thoughts and feelings in memoirs and other first-person genres (2013, 34). While Catholics could confess their sins to a priest and be absolved, Protestants were left to their own devices, and so, Heehs argues, many used their diaries as a way of confessing their sins directly to God (49). Heehs quotes a self-help book by John Beadle called *A Journal or Diary of a Thankful Christian* that was published in 1656 and recommends keeping a journal, because this,

> especially if we look often into it, and read it over will be a noteable means to increase in us that self-abasement & abhorrency of spirit that is most acceptable in the sight of God. ... Oh! How will the serious survey of such a Journal

DOI: 10.1057/9781137476661.0003

abase the soul before the Lord! Such a course would very much help our faith. (qtd by Heehs 2013, 51–2)

Although Heehs and Serfaty argue that diary-writing was important to Protestants in particular, writing about the self as a method for self-improvement was also part of Catholic traditions. For example, the Jesuits had a whole system of spiritual exercises intended to support followers in writing a narrative of their life that allowed them to understand themselves as sinners to become less sinful in the future (Molina 2008). This emphasis on sin is similar to what we saw in Heehs's quote from Beadle's book, and just as Beadle wrote a practical guide to diary-writing, the Jesuits had explicit guidelines for how to write spiritual narratives about oneself. J. Michelle Molina quotes a late sixteenth century description of the Spiritual Exercises that were initiated by St Ignatius, the founder of the Jesuit order:

Consideration of oneself. Tuesday. Points: consideration of self and of time and place: Where are you? Who are you? Also, reflection on each phase of your life: the time, the place, the state of life, circumstances in which he then lived as a sinner in each period; the things he happened to witness, and how swiftly and unmindfully everything passed by. His state of mind then and now. (2008, 289)

Although Christian traditions of writing about the self emphasised sin there was also room for joy and gratitude. Heehs sets the self-abasement in Beadle's book in contrast to today's self-affirmation (52), but reading through this best-selling seventeenth century guide on how to keep a spiritual journal, which has been digitised and can be read online, we discover that Beadle also writes a great deal about recording mercies, grace and deliverances, not just sin. Here are some of Beadle's notes (1656) about the importance of writing about the good in your life:

To keep a Journal or Diary, especially of God's gracious dealings with us, is a work, for a Christian singularly. ... It is good to keep an History, a Register, a Diary, an Annal not only of the places in which we have lived; but of the mercies that have been bellowed on us, continued to us all our dayes. ... Remember, and for that end put into your Journal all deliverances from dangers, vouchsafed to you or yours. And indeed, what is our whole life, but a continued deliverance?

A later, secular tradition of personal writing that also has influenced contemporary digital forms of self-expression is the commonplace book. In 1706 John Locke published a book explaining in detail how to organise a commonplace book, with an index to make it easier to relocate quotes and ideas. Ralph Waldo Emerson began to keep such a book, but fused

DOI: 10.1057/9781137476661.0003

it with the personal diary. Lawrence Rosenwald (1988) links this to the specifically American tradition of transcendentalism:

> Emerson has chosen to put in his diary not only the continuous record of his life and thought but also the thousand evanescent thoughts by which that record is complicated. In his book, that is, the private and public, the eternal and the contingent, the life and the work will inevitably collide and fuse. Losty speculations must be shown to have arisen in time, in a sequence of other events, from the mind of a particular human being. (59, qtd by Serfaty 2004, 46)

Samuel Pepys' diary is one of the first and certainly best known early secular diaries. He offers as much self-examination as the Puritans, but with less anguish, Heehs writes, citing an example where Pepys in great detail describes a quarrel with his wife without moralising or guilt (60–1). By the late eighteenth century diaries were common both in everyday life and in fiction, with several novels being written in the form of a diary.

Blogs and online diaries are obvious descendents of the diaries and autobiographies of past centuries. Filterblogs and topic-driven blogs (J.W. Rettberg 2014, 23–7) tend more towards the traditions of the commonplace book or the early Japanese diary tradition of *nikki bungaku*, which predates the Western diary by several centuries, but in which diaries tell of daily events and barely mention the writer (Heehs 2013, 9). Filter blogs often have a very personal style, much as Montaigne's essays did, but their aim is to share material and ideas that the blogger is interested in rather than to tell the story of the blogger's life. Personal blogs and online diaries are more unequivocally self-representations. The lines between a self-representational blog and one that is not self-representational are not always clear cut. A topic-driven blog (J.W. Rettberg 2014, 23–7) about fashion or the author's research will often mix posts about fashion or research in general with posts showing the blogger's 'outfit of the day' or the researcher's anxieties about finishing her PhD, topics which are clearly self-representational. Anonymous blogs may consist of nothing but captioned reaction gifs, and expose nothing of the author's identity, yet still express a personal experience of life.

Visual self-portraits in history

Centuries before Parmigianino's *Self-Portrait*, monks copying manuscripts would often draw small pictures of themselves in their texts, and artists would paint their own face on characters in paintings. In the eighteenth

DOI: 10.1057/9781137476661.0003

century artists' self-portraits became fashionable collectors' items, and towards the end of the twentieth century, artists have increasingly used their own bodies in their art.

Some of the most interesting pre-digital self-portraits in our context are those created by early photographers. Our digital cameras can slip into a pocket or be a lens tacked onto a mobile phone. The first cameras, on the other hand, were huge devices. Just as the camera taking the photograph is visible in digital self-portraits taken in a mirror, so early photographers often included the tool of their trade in their self-portraits. When included, the heavy cameras often appeared as powerful extensions of the photographer's body, as in Kate Matthew's *Self-portrait* (c. 1900, p 118 in Borzello's *Seeing Ourselves* [(Borzello, 1998]) or Margaret Bourke-White's *Self-portrait with Camera* (c. 1933, p 135 in Borzello). Alternatively, cameras were presented as barriers placed between the photographer and the audience, as in Germaine Krull's *Self-portrait with Cigarette and Camera* (1925, p 143 in Borzello). Ilse Bing, on the other hand, took self-portraits with a small, compact Leica, including herself, her camera and some of her surroundings and the mirror or other reflective surface she was using to take the photo, in works very reminiscent of today's mirror selfies. In *Self-portrait with Leica*, 1931 (p 142 in Borzello), Bing holds her small camera a little away from her face, looking just above and past the viewfinder at the spectator, or, as we realise, at herself in the mirror that enables the self-portrait. Another mirror is visible in the left of the picture, offering another view of Bing's face. Her face is serious yet intent, as we usually are when we look at ourselves in the mirror.

Decades later, many self-portraits showed still more fragmented versions of the self, tending to 'conceal or suppress the face and head, thereby thwarting traditional physiognomic/phrenological readings' (Hall 2013, chapter 10, para. 2). Rather than showing a single image of a head and shoulders, or perhaps a whole body, these images may show many fragmentary views (as in Nancy Kitchel's *My Face Covered Grandma's Gestures*, 1972–73, p 163 in Borzello) or they might show a full body shot again and again, changing a little over time, as in Eleanor Antin's *Carving: A Traditional Sculpture* (Borzello 1972, 162). As performance art and video art gained territory, self-portraits have become more and more common. Cindy Sherman uses her own image in most if not all of her artwork, posing in different roles. She claims these aren't self-portraits at all, but acting. Sometimes it is hard to draw the line. Perhaps they are a little of both.

DOI: 10.1057/9781137476661.0003

Today's selfies are different in that they are a true vernacular genre. They are rarely exhibited in art galleries; instead they are shared with friends and followers on social media. Although early photographers often used the camera as a barrier to protect them from the viewers in their self-portraits (Borzello 1998, 142), the classic outstretched arm of the selfie taken with a front-facing smart phone camera very strongly includes the viewer in the space of the photograph. As Katie Warwick points out, the outstretched arm is like a (forced) embrace, placing the viewer *between* the face of the person photographed and the camera (Warfield 2014).

The history of quantitative self-representation

My six-year-old runs to the window every time she hears a siren and looks for the number written on the side of the ambulance or fire engine. She has set up a siren-watching station with a pencil and paper at the ready by the window, and carefully writes down the numbers in the large, freshly learned script of a kindergartener. Sometimes the numbers are backwards, but she doesn't mind, she can read them. She has organised her log in two sections, one headed with a drawing of a fire engine and one with a drawing of an ambulance. Sometimes she point out patterns in her logs: 'Look, the ambulance with the number 33 on it went that way down the street and then it came back a bit later.' But mostly she seems simply to want to keep her logs perfectly up to date. 'I can't miss a siren, Mummy,' she explains at bedtime, leaping out of bed to maintain her perfect records.

If the mode of the diary is narrative, then the modes of quantitative self-representation are numbers, lists, maps and graphs. Before today's spreadsheets, activity trackers and GPS diaries, people used pens and paper to track their habits, their money, their sleep patterns and their travels. A prisoner scratching tally marks on the wall for each day of imprisonment is creating a form of quantitative diary, as is the teenager keeping a list of every book she has read or the father noting down the time when he puts his baby down to sleep and the time the baby wakes up.

The ways in which we have represented ourselves with numbers and data have been less studied than the histories of visual self-portraits and written autobiographies, memoirs and diaries, at least from the point of

DOI: 10.1057/9781137476661.0003

view of self-representation and aesthetics. Self-portraits and life-writing, on the other hand, are studied by art historians and literary historians, although unpublished or amateur works have been little discussed until the last few decades.

Benjamin Franklin (2007) was an early self-tracker. In his autobiography he wrote about how he tried to become a better person:

> It was about this time I conceiv'd the bold and arduous project of arriving at moral perfection. I wish'd to live without committing any fault at any time; I would conquer all that either natural inclination, custom, or company might lead me into. As I knew, or thought I knew, what was right and wrong, I did not see why I might not always do the one and avoid the other. (63)

Franklin chose 13 virtues he wanted to focus on and drew a chart with a column for each day of the week and a row for each virtue: temperance, silence, order, resolution, frugality, industry, sincerity, justice, moderation, cleanliness, chastity, tranquility and humility. He gave himself a black mark for each day he felt he hadn't lived up to each virtue, and two marks if he had done particularly badly. In the example he shows us in his autobiography we see that he had trouble with silence. He gave himself two black marks for silence on Sunday and one on Monday, Wednesday and Friday. Order was also a problem for him. In the week shown, Franklin was only satisfied with his sense of order on the Wednesday. He did quite well at resolution though, only failing at that on Tuesday and Friday.

This kind of habit tracking was used by many before Franklin and is popular today as well. We use star charts with our children and cross items off our to-do lists with satisfaction.

But self-tracking must have started far earlier than this. The first writing was developed not to record words and sentences but to keep accounts. Arguably, recording quantities of grain or other valuables can be a form of self-representation, or at least representation of what belongs to the self. Medieval annals of history sometimes listed years with no commentary: 726, 727, 728, 729 and 730. When words were used to describe a year, the words were brief, as for the year 709 in *Annales Sangallenses Maiores, dicti Hepidanni* of the *Monumenta Germaniae Historica* as quoted by Roberto Simanowski: 'Hard winter. Duke Gottfried died.' (2012, 20). Simanowski compares the way the *Annales* lists years and events without integrating them into a causal narrative with Facebook's automated Timeline (21), which likewise lists events without explanation or causal connections.

DOI: 10.1057/9781137476661.0003

Quantitative self-representation is pre- or post-narrative. Whether we look at Franklin's habit chart or my six-year-old's siren log there is no causal narrative to be seen. We may well infer causality (if the ambulance labelled 33 shows up twice in a row it was probably called out to a medical emergency and then returned to the hospital with the patient) but this requires interpretation. As the literary theorist Wolfgang Iser (1988) argued, we are good at reading more into a story than is written there. We fill in the gaps, what Iser called the *lehrstelle*, that are not explained in the story. Perhaps as we become more and more accustomed to reading quantitative representations, we will become even more adept a interpreting them as stories.

Literacy and access to writing materials were a pre-requisite for diary-writing. Quantitative self-representations are dependent on other forms of literacy: understanding counting, tables and graphs for instance. For digital forms of quantitative self-representation, we need to understand not only both these basic forms of numeracy and data literacy but also some procedural literacies (Mateas 2005). You don't need to be able to program to use an activity tracker or a lifelogging app, but certainly the most engaging examples of quantitative self-representation are produced by people who know how to access and manipulate their data, and also have the graphic design skills to present it in an appealing and effective way, like Nicholas Felton's annual reports or the examples reported daily at sites like Quantified Self and Flowing Data.

In the last few years, however, we have seen an ever-increasing number of consumer devices that automatically track our activity, posture, health and so on. One in ten adult Americans now owns an activity tracker. Quantitative self-representation is becoming commonplace.

Texts or people?

Self-representation with digital technologies is also self-documentation. We think not only about how to present ourselves to others, but also log or record moments of our lives for ourselves to remember them in the future. In her ongoing research on selfies, Katie Warfield notes that this is the first time we can use a device to simultaneously see our reflection and record it. Mirrors allowed us to see our own reflection, but not to record it. Cameras allowed us to record our own image, but until the digital display and front-facing camera of the smartphone, they did not allow

DOI: 10.1057/9781137476661.0003

us to see our face as we pressed the shutter (Warfield 2014). That, and the ease and inexpense of deleting digital images and taking new ones, allows us to control the way we are represented to a far greater degree than in a photobooth or holding an analogue camera up to a mirror. Writing a diary is also a way of externalising our thoughts and the way we see or think about ourselves. A private, paper diary may be written for a future self who will look back upon the time of writing. Although wearable devices like Fitbits or apps like Moves or Runkeeper generally suggest we share our steps or runs or productivity in social media, many (perhaps most) users prefer to keep their activity data private, or to only share some of it. When we share photos of our children or a new home or a night out with friends our target audience is not just our friends, but also ourselves.

Social media is about communication with others, but we should be equally aware of how we use social media to reflect upon ourselves. Creating and sharing a selfie is an act of self-representation – which as Gunn Enli and Nancy Thumin (2012) note, means that it involves the creation of *texts* which will be read and interpreted. A selfie also exists in a social context, once shared. But just as importantly, creating and sharing a selfie or a stream of selfies is a form of self-reflection and self-creation.

As readers, we encounter other people in social media as *texts*. From our perspective their self-expression is self-representation. This is particularly true when we are readers more than participants. Until the late 1990s, being on the Internet typically meant communicating with peers, on Usenet discussion forums, IRC, MUDs and MOOs. Early online diarying communities similarly emphasised the community and the social aspects of online diaries. In her study of Internet users' experience of being online, Annette Markham (1998) discusses the relationship between our bodies and the virtual online experience. There weren't many photographs on the Internet in the 1990s. Few people had digital cameras or scanners, and download speeds were so slow that images took a long time to load anyway, so our bodies for the most part were hidden. We imagined that the Internet was disembodied, anonymous and virtual. It wasn't until the late 1990s and early 2000s that webcams became popular (Senft 2008), and we began to communicate with each other visually as well as through text. The shift to the visual on the Internet and especially in social media has increased a lot since then. Facebook was originally created to show photos of peoples' faces, and

DOI: 10.1057/9781137476661.0003

today shared images are central to most social media. Our bodies are no longer hidden online.

Images are the primary content of many services such as Instagram, Pinterest, Snapchat and We Heart It. The earlier Internet, on the other hand, relied on words and conversations. People who just watched and read and didn't participate were given the derogatory term *lurker*, and it was clear that the expectation was active participation. Seeing yourself as a peer communicating with others was key to your identity online, Markham wrote: 'through conversations, self and reality are co-created and sustained' (1998, 227). We 'write self into being,' but to 'recognize our own existence in any meaningful way, we must be responded to' (Markham 2013a).

When we write and share photos with our friends on Facebook we primarily see the social communication we are engaging in, rather than the text of their and our own self-representations. But when we merely lurk or follow, we position ourselves as traditional readers, as voyeurs, as an audience – and from this point of view, we analyse the other writer primarily as a text rather than as a living, breathing human being. This is the perspective from which selfies and other forms of online self-expression primarily become self-representations.

Interestingly, some social media sites and apps make it hard to directly communicate with each other, foregrounding the *text* rather than the conversation or the speakers. We Heart It is an Instagram-like photosharing space that does not allow commenting and only allows users to interact by 'hearting' each other's images. Tumblr doesn't allow direct conversational comments; instead you have to reblog a post on your own Tumblr blog and add notes to it there. This means that only your own followers and not all followers of the original poster will automatically see your notes, and although most Tumblr users write under a pseudonym, it means that anything you write on another user's blog also shows up on your own Tumblr blog.

On the other hand, older forms of online communication such as Usenet discussion groups, MUDs and MOOs or IRC positioned all participants as peers. Each person's words were presented in the same font, in the same manner and made visible to all subscribers, to all players in the same room or to all users in the same channel. Private person-to-person conversation was also possible in many of these earlier communication spaces. For instance, a player in a MUD could whisper something to another character, and other players would only see a

DOI: 10.1057/9781137476661.0003

message such as 'X whispers something to Y' and only Y would see the content of the message. And of course, in all communication spaces, if users give each other their contact information in another medium (email, telephone, messaging) private communication can be conducted outside of the more public space.

Twitter is an interesting in-between form. On the one hand, every user's posts are presented in exactly the same manner, in a continuous feed that is not dissimilar to the chat interface of a MOO or IRC conversation in the mid-nineties. Using @replies and direct messages people have conversations, and hashtags allow conversations about shared interests to take place between strangers, much as we used to see on Usenet or IRC. On the other hand, every tweet is stored, and you can go back and read all tweets from a particular user in order, as though they are a text. Some users have millions of followers while others have barely any, and it is easy to 'lurk' and read other peoples' tweets without responding to them or in any way making yourself known to the tweeter. It is possible to use Twitter for communication between equals or to be a broadcaster or an audience. In the latter case, a reader – and perhaps also the writer – will see other users' tweets as *text*, as self-representations rather than as self-expression. The same tweets may be primarily experienced as social communication by other users who engage in conversation with the tweeter, and the tweeter himself or herself may see them primarily as self-exploration and not even really care whether he or she receives any response to them.

An example of the mismatch between seeing a stream of tweets as text rather than as self-expression can be seen in the frequent condemnation of people who tweet or blog or in other ways share stories of illness or hardship in social media. Lisa Boncheck Adams (@AdamsLisa) is a mother of three who tweets and blogs about her life with cancer, in effect writing what G. Thomas Couser (2012) in his categorisation of memoirs would call an autopathography. In mid-January 2014 Adams was undergoing radiation treatment and frequently posted about the pain of side effects, with fairly detailed descriptions of the mundane mechanics of undergoing this kind of treatment:

> Pain today is worst in days. Cannot get on top of it. I have 1)constant drip plus ability to do 2)on-demand drip, 3)emergency. All in use. (@AdamsLisa, 8 Jan 2014)

There is more to Adams' Twitter stream than blow by blow descriptions of treatment, though. Many of her posts are humorous, similar to her 16

DOI: 10.1057/9781137476661.0003

December tweet: 'In the Cancer Olympics there would be a medal for contrast chugging #contender', where the tweet was accompanied by a photo of a jug of red contrast liquid. And each morning she posts the same words as an inspirational call to focus on what is beautiful: 'Find a bit of beauty in the world today. Share it. If you can't find it, create it. Some days this may be hard to do. Persevere.' Importantly, more than half of her tweets are conversational and directly addressed to other users.

Adams came to international media attention after two opinion pieces about the way she tweeted about her illness were published, one by Emma Keller (2014) in *The Guardian* and one by Bill Keller (2014), Emma's husband, in *The New York Times*. The two pieces received a great deal of criticism in social media for their judgement of Adams, and Emma Keller's piece was removed from *The Guardian* a few days later (Elliott 2014).

Emma and Bill Keller explicitly place themselves in the role of traditional audience to Adams' tweets. Instead of participating in the conversation and seeing themselves as Adams' peers or friends, they are readers of a text, members of a large audience watching a performance: 'Her decision to live her cancer onstage invites us to think about it, debate it, learn from it,' Bill Keller (2014) writes, and his use of the term 'onstage' is revealing. He sees Adams primarily as a performer, not as a peer. 'Look how swiftly the logic sweeps from "her decision" to "our debates,"' Megan Garber (2014) wrote in *The Atlantic*. In this way Keller goes from considering Adams as a living person to seeing her (or at least her tweets) as a text to be analysed and criticised from outside just like any other text or performance. Similarly, Emma Keller's piece in *The Guardian* (since retracted) asked questions from the viewpoint of an audience: 'Should there be boundaries in this kind of experience? Is there such a thing as TMI? Are her tweets a grim equivalent of deathbed selfies, one step further than funeral selfies? Why am I so obsessed?' (E. Keller 2014)

What this approach forgets is that the texts we read in real time in social media represent actual, living people. This is not like writing about a movie or a novel and its fictional characters. It is not even like writing about a movie star or politician, although they of course are also actual, living people. Perhaps Adams could be called a micro-celebrity (Senft 2008, 25–8; Senft 2013), especially after the attention from international news media which led to a rapid increase in followers and readers. But as Alice Marwick (2013) writes, 'the idea of using the tools of celebrity

DOI: 10.1057/9781137476661.0003

culture to analyze the lives of regular people is problematic because the protections available to mainstream celebrities do not exist for micro-celebrities.' Micro-celebrities do not have agents and PR consultants to protect them from the press and the public.

In both the Kellers' opinion pieces they criticised Adams for how frequently she tweets. Bill Keller's *The New York Times* article begins thus,

> LISA BONCHEK ADAMS has spent the last seven years in a fierce and very public cage fight with death. Since a mammogram detected the first toxic seeds of cancer in her left breast when she was 37, she has blogged and tweeted copiously about her contest with the advancing disease. She has tweeted through morphine haze and radiation burn. Even by contemporary standards of social-media self-disclosure, she is a phenomenon. (Last week she tweeted her 165,000th tweet.)

In the piece, Keller stresses that Adams is 'very public', that she blogs and tweets 'copiously' and is a phenomenon 'even by contemporary standards of social-media disclosure.' The condemnation, almost ridicule, is clear, and one of the reasons she is caricatured in this way is that she speaks too much. 165,000 tweets.

Adams herself insists on being read differently. Despite being in hospital when the opinion pieces came out, Adams responded, writing among other things:

> My tweet count is not high because I only churn out tweets. It's conversation. Talking. Asking people how they are... And listening for answer. (@AdamsLisa, 14 Jan 2014)

Looking at her Twitter stream it is clear that Adams is right: she places a lot of emphasis on answering tweets from other people and on participating in a conversation. She uses Twitter as a social space for conversation and as a diary, although she certainly also has many followers who don't participate in the conversation.

1305 of the 2402 tweets Adams posted between 15 December 2013 and 15 January 2014 were @replies: they were messages directly addressed to other users. That means that more than half of her tweets were conversational. This is not just Adams talking with a small network of friends. Adams' @replies are addressed to 457 different users, so she participates in a very broad conversation. Her 165,000 tweets do not mean she has written an extremely long text, they mean that she is participating daily in conversations with others.

DOI: 10.1057/9781137476661.0003

But of course there is a difference between reading posts from a person we know and care about and reading those of a stranger. And it is natural that Emma and Bill Keller read Adams' tweets with their own response and feelings about the tweets foremost in their minds. We are all at the centre of our own world.

Disciplining self-representations

The Kellers' condemnation of Lisa Adams is very similar to the disgust that is shown for selfies in the mainstream media. Anne Burns' excellent research blog *The Carceral Net: Photography, Feminism and Social Media's Disciplinary Principle* (2013–ongoing) documents and analyses many examples of selfie hatred, for instance in 'Selfies and Hatred' (23 May 2014) and 'Selfies and Hatred, Part 2' (30 June 2014).

Some of the hatred is quite direct, such as the t-shirts with the slogan 'Go fuck your #selfie', or the PBS YouTube video 'Why Do We Hate Selfies?' that normalises the hatred. Other times the disdain for selfies is slightly more subtle, as with the media stories that abounded in April and May 2014 about selfies being a symptom of narcissism, or the idea that selfie-takers need to be helped, for instance made over Pygmalion-style by a benevolent man as in the autumn 2014 ABC TV series 'Selfie'. Anne Burns analyses the trailer for the series in her post 'My Fair Selfie' on 30 May 2014. Ridicule is another approach, and it is for instance seen in the Chainsmokers' video #SELFIE, which Burns discusses in her 2 May 2014 blog post 'The Curious Confusion of #Selfie'. Here women are shown in the bathroom having vapid conversations about men and dresses and repeating the chorus, 'First, let me take a selfie.'

Burns sees the hatred, ridicule and pathologising as mechanisms that society uses to discipline the stereotypical selfie-takers: young women. We saw the same mechanism in the early days of blogging. I began blogging in my late twenties as a PhD student and was often called an exhibitionist or narcissist by non-blogging colleagues (Mortensen and Walker 2002; Walker 2006). I wrote a blog post about this on 24 July 2001, where I accepted the label but asked, 'Why are we so afraid of being thought exhibitionists, anyway?' I quoted Nancy K. Miller's book on personal criticism where she writes about how her mother would deride other women with the condemning words 'She's making a spectacle of herself!' Women have been conditioned not to expose themselves,

DOI: 10.1057/9781137476661.0003

I argued. We've been taught to hide; to be ashamed of 'overly rouged cheeks, of a voice shrill in laughter, or of a sliding bra strap – a loose, dingy bra strap especially' (Miller 1991, 23). Of course, blogging and selfies are not phenomena that are exclusive to women – far from it – but the accusation of blogging or selfies as being narcissistic or exhibitionistic is particularly common when women engage in these practices.

When teenage girls became the most popular and financially successful bloggers in Norway and Sweden towards the end of the first decade of this millennium, they were met by the same disdain as selfies are met with today (Dmitrow-Devold 2013, Palmgren 2010). It is true that the most successful of these blogs were not about the sorts of topics typically seen as valuable by mainstream journalists or arguably by most adults: they were mostly fashion or makeup blogs, full of photos of daily outfits and fashion advice, although the bloggers also sometimes wrote about humanitarian causes or other political issues, and negotiate what Mia Lövheim (2011) calls 'ethical spaces' through their blogging. Today the most successful Norwegian blogs are run by young women and have more daily readers than most Norwegian newspapers. Regardless of the content, it is striking that when young women in their teens and early twenties for the first time have found platforms that allow them to speak without censorship to large public audiences, society's kneejerk reaction is to mock them.

Many scholars, including Anne Burns, have used Michel Foucault's writings about discipline and power to analyse the ways in which mockery, hatred and pathologising are used as disciplinary strategies to put young women in particular back in their place. This is about power and about who has the right to speak in public or to share images in public.

We don't mind so much when celebrities share selfies, as when Ellen DeGeneres shot the famous group selfie of movie stars at the 2014 Oscars. We don't even mind it when people who already have an audience through traditional media tweet about illness and death. When NPR reporter Scott Simon live-tweeted his mother's last days at the end of July 2013, there was a little discussion about whether this was insensitive, or whether it invaded his mother's privacy, or whether Simon could be fully present in the moment with his mother if he was also tweeting. Overall, though, comments were very supportive, and we saw no sustained criticism in major mainstream media. Simon's tweets shared a deep grief, immediately felt:

DOI: 10.1057/9781137476661.0003

You wake up and realize: you weren't dreaming. It happened. Cry like you couldn't last night. @nprscottsimon 7:14 AM – 30 July 2013

Mother cries Help Me at 2;30. Been holding her like a baby since. She's asleep now. All I can do is hold on to her. (@nprscottsimon 5:35 am, 29 July 2013)

Mother asks, 'Will this go on forever?' She means pain, dread. 'No.' She says, 'But we'll go on forever. You & me.' Yes. (@nprscottsimon 11:07 PM – 27 July 2013)

Unlike Lisa Adams, Scott Simon was already a well-established journalist with more than a million followers on Twitter. He already had a public persona, so this series of tweets didn't define him.

In 1960, Abbott Joseph Liebling wrote that 'Freedom of the press is guaranteed only to those who own one.' Today you don't need to own a printing press, a newspaper or a television station to share your ideas with the world. Anyone with Internet access can publish whatever they want. But society is finding new ways to regulate who will be heard and who will be taken seriously.

In her article 'Me and My Shadow,' Jane Tompkins (1989) asked 'How can we speak personally to one another and not be self-centred?' I think the answer is in the words 'one another'. That is what the Kellers' criticisms of Lisa Adams tweets about cancer miss, and that is what my colleagues missed about my blogging with other PhD students in my field in the early 2000s, and it is what is missed in the hatred and ridicule of selfies. These aren't simply texts published from a distance. They are images and words that are part of a conversation.

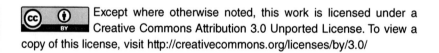

DOI: 10.1057/9781137476661.0003

OPEN

2

Filtered Reality

Abstract: *This chapter proposes using the term 'filter' as an analytical term to understand algorithmic culture. In everyday speech, we filter our photos and filter our news. In today's algorithmic culture the filter has become a pervasive metaphor for the ways in which technology can remove certain content and how it can alter or distort texts, images and data. Filters can be technological, cultural or cognitive, or they can be a combination of these. Examples discussed are the skin tone bias in photography, Instagram filters and the genres of social media as filters that embed a drive towards progress, and baby journals and the apps that automate them.*

Rettberg, Jill Walker. *Seeing Ourselves Through Technology: How We Use Selfies, Blogs and Wearable Devices to See and Shape Ourselves.* Basingstoke: Palgrave Macmillan, 2014. DOI: 10.1057/9781137476661.0004.

DOI: 10.1057/9781137476661.0004

Filters have become an important part of popular visual culture. Insta-gram was one of the first sites to really popularise filters, and now they are everywhere, allowing us to make our selfies and other photos look brighter, more muted, more grungy, or more retro than real life. We don't just filter our images before we post them to Instagram, though: filter has become an important and far more general concept in today's digital culture. We filter our images, our email and our newsfeeds.

In academia, we have been used to talking about how any technol-ogy comes with certain affordances and constraints. In an algorithmic culture where we have far more data than we can possibly use, we need to start thinking more about how algorithms filter our content, remov-ing or altering our data. We need to think about how these filters work. What is filtered out? What flavours or styles are added?

The word filter has been used in many domains, but usually to describe a process where something is removed. A filter can be a piece of felt or a piece of paper which filters out dust, dirt or other impurities when water is poured through it or air blows through it. A screen can filter out certain colours in light. On a cigarette a filter stops some of the harmful substances from reaching the smoker's lungs. In electronics a filter is 'A passive circuit that attenuates all signals except those within one or more frequency bands,' the Oxford English Dictionary (OED) states. In radiology a filter can block out certain wavelengths in an x-ray beam. In March 2014, the OED published a draft definition of the word filter as used in computing: 'To process or reformat (data) using a filter esp. so as to remove unwanted content.' Instagram filters are not mentioned. Instead the examples given refer to filtering your email, filtering the results from sports events and filtering performance data to compare it with other data.

It is interesting that all the definitions and examples the OED lists for filter as a noun or as a verb emphasise the removal of unwanted content or impurities. Instagram filters may in fact remove data, for instance by making a colour image black and white, but often the perceived effect is of adding to the image: boosting the colours, adding borders, creating a vignette effect or blurring parts of the image. A coffee filter does some-thing similar, though coffee filters are not mentioned in the OED's list of usages for filter. Technically the coffee filter does stop the ground coffee beans from getting into the pot beneath, but the *point* of a coffee filter is to add flavour to water by slowing its flow through the coffee beans.

Filters can get worn out or clogged up over time, letting more particles through than before, or altering the flow of the water, air, rays or words,

DOI: 10.1057/9781137476661.0004

images, numbers and behaviours that pass through them. We can change, clean, adapt, resist or remove filters. But most of the time we simply take them for granted, not even noticing that they are there.

Technological and cultural filters

By using the popular cultural term 'filter' as an analytical term, I want to emphasise the similarities between the visual filters we apply to our photographs, the technological filters we apply to our blogs and other social media feeds and the cultural filters (norms, expectations, normative discursive strategies) that teach us, for instance, to mimic photo models in fashion magazines or Instagram selfie stars when we photograph ourselves.

The terms we use to analyse our world and our culture matter. As Kenneth Burke wrote,

> Not only does the nature of our terms affect the nature of our observations, in the sense that the terms direct the attention to one field rather than to another. Also, many of the 'observations' are but implications of the particular terminology in terms of which the observations are made. In brief, much that we take as observations about 'reality' may be but the spinning out of possibilities implicit in our particular choice of terms. (1968, 46)

Burke wrote about 'terministic screens', the terms in our language through which our understanding of the world is filtered (Markham 2013b). Language can certainly be understood as a technology, and it is another of the filters that surround us. Using the term filter to understand today's digital culture is a conscious choice: let us use the terms that are popular in our culture to understand it.

In her 2007 book *Mediated Memories*, José van Dijck writes about '*normative discursive strategies* that either implicitly or explicitly structure our agencies,' giving pre-formatted baby journals as an example (7). A preformatted baby journal can be seen as a technological filter. It is a conventional codex book, which means you cannot easily add very large photos or video or sound, and it has written prompts and spaces allocated to specific kinds of photographs. You can tear out pages or glue photographs over prompts you don't want to use, but the journal does provide very clear rules for how you should represent your baby's first year.

DOI: 10.1057/9781137476661.0004

An app like Sprout Baby (for iPhone and iPad by Med ART Studios) provides even clearer rules. Baby journals have always had an element of quantitative tracking: it is common to include dated notes about achievements (first smile, first steps), weight and height charts and even information about which teeth came in on which date. But Sprout Baby encourages even more detailed tracking, letting parents track each feeding, each nappy change and each nap. Sprout Baby also prompts parents to add photos of milestones: First Smile, Found His Hands and Feet, Laughed Out Loud and so on. The iPad version of the app generates a newspaper style layout of all the latest journal notes, photos and numbers under the title (for a baby named Jack) 'Jack Today' in a newspaper-style headline font. Personal data, notes and photos are combined with standard advice to parents with babies of this age, for instance as shown in the demonstration screenshots in the iTunes store: 'Baby and household chores can add up. Make sure you divvy up the load by listing everything you need to do and dividing it equally so no one is trying to handle more than their share.'

Sprout Baby App is an example of how an app can streamline and limit our options for personal expression even more than pre-digital media. A pre-formatted baby journal may constrain our creativity, but Sprout app does so even more. You cannot tear out a page or glue an extra photograph over pixels.

Technological filters allow us to express ourselves in certain ways but not in others. We can apply certain filters to an image we post to Instagram but not others. We can post animated gifs to Tumblr or Reddit but not to Facebook, although this may change. With Photoshop or programming skills and a self-hosted website of course we can express ourselves in other ways, but most of us do not have these resources and simply choose between different available filters. Twitter filters out long form writing, requiring us to limit ourselves to 140 characters at a time. Reddit uses upvotes and downvotes to filter out posts and comments that are not popular with a large number of its users. You can still see the posts if you dig deep enough, but not as easily. If we follow Alice Marwick's (2013) argument in her ethnography of developers of social media in Silicon Valley, we could say that social media in general filters out people who are not effective neoliberal subjects. Perhaps in this case, social media is not simply the kind of filter that removes impurities, but also shapes them and flavours people as the ground coffee beans flavour the water that passes through them. An effective neoliberal subject,

DOI: 10.1057/9781137476661.0004

Marwick argues, 'attends to fashions, is focused on self-improvement, and purchases goods and services to achieve "self-realization." He or she is comfortable integrating market logics into many aspects of life, including education, parenting, and relationships. In other words, the ideal neoliberal citizen is an entrepreneur' (2013, 13). These are the people most likely to succeed in social media, most likely to gain followers on Twitter and most likely to have their Facebook posts filtered into your newsfeed.

In the July 2014 debates around the 'emotional contagion' experiment in which nearly 700,000 Facebook users were shown posts including more or less positive words than previously (Kramer, Guillory and Hancock 2014), we learned that this minor tweak to the way in which the newsfeed filters our friends' posts actually changed the users' own status updates. Users who saw posts with more positive words used more positive words in their own posts, and vice versa. Whether this affected users' actual emotional state or not, it is clear that the way Facebook filters our newsfeeds affects the way we express ourselves on Facebook. Facebook filters our newsfeed, and it also filters our behaviour.

Cultural filters are as important as technological filters. Our cultural filters, the rules and conventions that guide us, filter out possible modes of expression so subtly that we often are not even aware of all the things we do not see. Whether we create a baby journal for our baby's first year or not, most parents will take photos of certain moments. There'll be photos of the newborn baby, photos of the baby smiling, the baby with its first tooth, the baby crawling, walking and of course its first birthday, preferably showing baby with the birthday cake. We filter out many of the other aspects of life with a baby when we create a photo album. Usually we will not take as many photos of the baby screaming, of endless nights trying to get the baby to go back to sleep, of the baby in a onesie that has spitup all over it although baby has only worn it for an hour. Partly this is because we would prefer to remember the good moments, but it is also because we know what we are supposed to document from having seen other baby journals and photo albums and from having seen which photographs and stories our friends and family share with us, offline or on social media. Our shared ideas about what moments and milestones should be documented in life act as a cultural filter that affects our choices.

We cannot represent our lives or our bodies without using or adapting, resisting and pushing against filters that are already embedded in

DOI: 10.1057/9781137476661.0004

our culture, whether those filters are cultural or technological. Cultural filters change over time and are different in different cultures. We can and often do resist or change cultural filters, but most of the time we simply act according to the logic of the filter without even realising that that is what we are doing.

Aestheticising, anesthetising and defamiliarising

Photo filters have become a cultural phenomenon that goes far beyond social media. Many photojournalists for mainstream media have taken to using smartphones and filters in their work, both as an aesthetic choice and because the look of a quick, filtered smartphone photo carries with it a sense of realism that documentary photographers may desire.

The millions of people on Instagram and other photo sharing sites may have no qualms in editing their photos, but photojournalists and theorists do sometimes object. In an article discussing the ways in which Instagram-style filters have been applied to photojournalism, Meryl Alper (2013) writes that

> Lowy's concession to his critics – 'toning down' the illustrative style of the very Hipstamatic photo filters that won him acclaim – touches upon an endless discussion about understanding all photography as a manipulated interaction between style and substance, and a timeless debate over the ethics of combining photojournalism with aesthetics. ... [S]cholars such as Luc Boltanski (1999) have argued that the aestheticization of what we see in the media emotionally and morally insulates viewers from the suffering of others.

In a project such as #365grateful, where participants share daily photographs of something they are grateful for, aestheticising the everyday is an explicit goal: a method to become more mindful of our daily experiences. Beauty can be seen in anything, and we can learn to be grateful for anything: after all, we are lucky to have clothes that need washing and should be grateful if we have a family to create that untidy mess of shoes in the hallway. When we see our pile of dirty laundry framed in a photograph we may be better able to see the beauty of the bright colours, and if it does not look beautiful to us, we can easily add a filter to the photograph to enhance its aesthetic qualities.

The photo filter both aestheticises and perhaps, as Sontag wrote of images of war , the filter anesthetises our everyday lives (1973, 20). At the

DOI: 10.1057/9781137476661.0004

same time filters show us images that look *different* than the world we are used to seeing.

One reason the filter fascinates us is that it gives the image that strangeness that defamiliarises our lives. The filter makes it clear that the image is not entirely ours. The filtered image shows us ourselves, or our surroundings, with a machine's vision. As Bianca Bosker (2014) writes about the wearable lifelogging camera the Narrative Clip, it 'lets me see my life through someone else's eyes – or in this case, the unfocused and impartial eye of a machine'.

In saying that filters 'defamiliarise' our lives I am referencing Victor Shklovsky, a literary theorist who wrote an influential article in 1917 titled 'Art as Technique'. Shklovsky argued that 'defamiliarisation' (*ostranenie* in the original Russian) is the key device in literature and art. 'Habitualization devours works, clothes, furniture, one's wife, and the fear of war,' Shklovsky (1988) wrote, and continued,

> The purpose of art is to impart the sensation of things as they are perceived and not as they are known. The technique of art is to make objects 'unfamiliar', to make forms difficult, to increase the difficulty and length of perception because the process of perception is an aesthetic end in itself and must be prolonged.

Instagram-style filters may make our selfies and photos of our everyday life seem unfamiliar, but the filter itself is repeated so often that the defamiliarisation effect wears off and becomes a cliché. For the most part, however, our everyday photos are not intended as art. They are a way of heightening our own daily experiences and making them special to ourselves. Shklovsky (1988) wrote, 'After we see an object several times, we begin to recognize it. The object is in front of us and we know about it, but we do not see it – hence we cannot say anything significant about it. Art removes objects from the automatism of perception in several ways.'

When we take a selfie (or any photograph) with a phone, the phone suggests running it through a filter. After Instagram and apps like Hipstamatic popularised filters, almost every camera or photo sharing app now comes with built-in filters. When you snap a photo on your iPhone, there is a filter icon at the bottom of the screen. When you upload a photo to Instagram, Facebook or Flickr you click through a screen that asks whether you want to filter it, crop it and adorn it. Taken together, filtered selfies are clichés. But for each individual *me*, seeing ourselves though a filter allows us to see ourselves anew.

DOI: 10.1057/9781137476661.0004

Selfies can be raw and revealing. They can feel too authentic, too honest. Perhaps running them through a filter to boost the colours, overexpose the skin to hide its imperfections or give them a retro tinge is sometimes the only way we can bear to share these images of ourselves. Putting a filter on our selfies, or framing them by placing them in a blog or an Instagram feed, gives them a distance that makes them new to us. We see ourselves and our surroundings as if we are outside of ourselves, through a retro filter or in the same poses and layouts as we see fashion models or homes in magazine spreads.

Choosing what technology can do

Filters can appear to be deeply technological: a new iPhone can count our steps with its M7 or M8 motion sensor and its accelerometer, gyroscope and compass, and it can use its microphone to measure how loud our surroundings are, but it cannot measure – at least not directly – our emotions. Our cameras know when we point them at a face, and can even wait until the person smiles before shooting a photo, but they cannot measure whether we love that person or not. Our bodies themselves are technologies with their own constraints and affordances: we can see colours and use language but cannot hear as well as dogs or navigate using biomagnetism and sonar as whales and dolphins do. Our brains and senses filter our perception of the world. In addition to technological and cultural filters, we have these cognitive filters that we cannot completely escape, although drugs, diseases, surgical implants and body modifications can alter them to some extent.

Individual devices have technological filters that are themselves influenced by cultural filters. For instance, an iPhone can track motion but not heart rate or the sweatiness of the palm holding it. It could have been designed differently, and we can study reasons why the choice has been made to build it only to perceive certain inputs. Of course cost and technological development are very important factors in determining what kinds of technological filters are built into a device, but many technological filters, whether they are built into hardware or software, are very deliberate cultural choices. For instance, the creators of the app SkinneePix, which lets you take selfies that show you looking skinnier than you are, wrote in a comment to an article about the app in *The Guardian* on 4 April 2014: 'We developed SkinneePix as a result of friends (mostly

DOI: 10.1057/9781137476661.0004

women, some overweight, some not) who would say: "Use the Skinny lens" when taking photos. So we made "the skinny lens." ' The results are not necessarily as flattering as the developers' friends might have hoped, but the idea of the 'skinny lens' is an example of how we are aware that technology filters our visual representations, just as Parmigianino highlighted the distortions in the self-portrait I described at the beginning of this book. There are many other apps similar to SkinneePix that will let you make your eyes bigger or your waist thinner or your skin more even.

Many filters are both technological and cultural, and often we are not aware of these filters. An example that is particularly relevant for selfies and photography in general is that of the bias towards white skin in most twentieth-century photography (Roth 2009; McFadden 2014). Early camera film was calibrated to provide good detail for white faces, but the light sensitivity was so narrow that faces with darker skin were shown with hardly any detail, with eyes and teeth often the only discernable features. Lighting and balance were calibrated by using 'Shirley cards': images of a pale skinned woman with dark hair against a white background. It is only in the last couple of decades that calibration cards have reflected all skin tones, for instance by including images of a range of people with different skin tones, as well as objects in a range of colours. Even today it can be difficult to take a photo of a light skinned and a dark skinned person together without losing all detail in one or the other face.

Lorna Roth writes that in the 1950s some parents did complain to Kodak that class photos lit for the white children did not show the faces of the black children, but despite this there were no organised campaigns for Kodak or other companies to improve film. It wasn't until the 1970s, when companies selling chocolate and dark woods complained that they couldn't get good photos of these dark items that Kodak developed their Gold Max film with better light sensitivity. Roth (2009) speculates that the reason that the change came from pressure from advertisers' rather than from the African-American community was that 'at the time, it was assumed by the public that such things were based on science and could not be changed, and so battles were fought on issues of economics, poverty, and other civil rights matters that were of higher priority to the African-American and African-Canadian communities' (120). This kind of technological determinism (the belief that technology drives cultural change) is a common assumption, often criticised by scholars but still

DOI: 10.1057/9781137476661.0004

frequently taken for granted by everyday people who have not had the assumption challenged (Winner 1980; Wyatt 2007). Photographers and the people who developed the technology were not likely to be deliberately creating the skin tone bias, at least not on an individual level, but the effect was far-reaching: people with darker skin tones rarely saw good or natural photographic images of themselves. And nobody thought of simply calibrating film to suit dark skin better. Even today, lighting and photography techniques tend to be taught to suit light skin tones, and as photographer Syreeta McFadden writes in her article 'Teaching The Camera to See My Skin' (2014), the skill of photographing people of colour well is often hard-learned and self-taught.

The skin tone bias of photography is a technological filter that distorts photographic representations of many people, but it isn't just about technology. The common stereotypical drawings of Africans in the mid-twentieth century show that the visual distortion was not just embedded into camera technology, it was also a strong cultural filter. In many ways, the skin tone bias in cameras is equivalent to an Instagram filter, but not a flattering one – rather, this filter dehumanises people. And importantly, it wasn't, and isn't, a filter we *choose* to apply, it is a filter or distortion that is almost inescapable using conventional technology.

Feeling misrepresented by the camera is one common reason for beginning to take selfies instead of being the subject of other people's photographs. Photographer McFadden (2014) describes how one of her driving motivations to begin taking self-portraits and to become a professional photographer was her horror at seeing photographs of herself:

> I couldn't help but feel that what that photographer saw was so wildly different from how I saw myself. Is that how you see me? Could you not see blackness? Its varying tones and textures? And do you see all of us that way?...I started taking pictures to self protect. I just couldn't bear seeing anymore shitty pictures of me. I didn't know what I wanted these images to say, but I knew I could make something beautiful.

Comments to another article on the same topic in the online magazine *Jezebel* (Stewart 2014) speak of similar experiences and motivations, as commenters talk about their dislike of the 'skin tone bias filter' as an explicit motivation for taking selfies. One commenter writes,

> Growing up all of my girlfriends (and immediate female relatives) were white. I would watch them effortlessly take a photo or get their photo taken and in

DOI: 10.1057/9781137476661.0004

return get an image that looked just like them. I never really felt that way. I still don't – unless I take my own photo. And people call it vanity but really I just want to be able to see myself in a picture. I don't see myself in other people's photos, I just don't.

Another commenter responds:

I've always felt this way too. Some people laugh at me for wanting to take selfies rather than have someone take the photo but I've always felt kind of shitty pre smartphone era when the photos would come back developed and I just woudn't look like me.

For McFadden and the commenters, taking selfies can be a way of avoiding cultural and technological filters that you don't like or that don't represent you in a way that feels real to you.

Genres as filters

Another kind of filter is the genre. When we choose to share our stories in a photo album or a blog or a handwritten diary or a pre-formatted baby journal, these choices carry with them sets of genre expectations. Some of the rules of a genre are flexible while others are absolute requirements. A photo album is not a photo album if there are no photos in it, and it is not a family photo album if all the photos are of landscapes.

Not all the rules in a genre are as obvious as photo albums requiring photos. For example, a blog must have dated posts in reverse chronological order (Walker 2005a, 45), but beyond these formal rules there are more subtle expectations that *can* be rejected but usually are not. Diane Greco noted in her blog, *Narcissism, vanity, exhibitionism, ambition, vanity, vanity, vanity*, on 25 February 2004, that the ongoingness of diet blogs (and by extension, any other blog with a goal) requires them to aim for success.

By and large, the blogs tell success stories. They have to – blogging as a literary form supports the idea of eventual success. When there's bad news from the bathroom scale, the open-endedness of blogging makes it possible to cast the gain as just a temporary setback, not a failure. Diet blogging recasts or reimagines the yo-yo effects of a diet as a surface, a space, a site for potentially endless re-inscription. Dieting as Etch-a-Sketch, very postmodern.

So long as the blog is not ended or deleted, any setback can only be a step on the way to some as yet unknown future. I discussed goal-oriented

DOI: 10.1057/9781137476661.0004

narratives and the ongoing and episodic narration of blogs in the chapter on blogs as narratives in my book *Blogging* (2014). Blogs are written in real-time, and therefore, unlike the narratives in many novels, the narrator usually doesn't know what is in the future. But many bloggers do write about clear goals, hopes or dreams.

Facebook functions as a filter that echoes this story of constant progress, especially with the strong structure embedded in the life events in its Timeline. As Roberto Simanowski (2012) points out, Facebook lists weight loss as a kind of life event you can add to your time, but it doesn't list weight gain. It suggests you might like to add quitting a habit to your Timeline as a life event, but does not suggest sharing that you have started a habit (23).

The progress narrative can be inverted, as in the many communities online where people support each other in what mainstream society sees as destructive practices. While a diet blog may always point towards an imagined future success, pro-anorexia blogs are examples of a drive to self-improvement that can become dangerous. If you look at the recently published photos on a visual social network site such as We Heart It, you will quickly see that popular images include not only beautiful photos with inspirational quotes about love and beauty but also a great many melancholy images with superimposed texts about depression, heartbreak and anxiety. The site We Heart It was actually designed to avoid online bullying and negativity: there is no option to comment on images and the only act a user can take is to upload an image or to 'heart' an image. But many images either include text or consist of nothing but text, of course saved as an image file so as to fit the format of the site – effectively circumventing the technological filter of not allowing text that the site apparently intended. The progress narratives of social media can be inverted, with progress still a drive that calls for more and more, but where that 'more' may lead to ever stronger depression, self-harm or hatred of others.

A filtered world

I have used the term filter in different ways in this chapter. I began by talking about literal filters: the felt or paper that water is filtered through to remove impurities and the piece of coloured glass that blocks certain frequencies of light. I moved on to talk about technological filters, ways

DOI: 10.1057/9781137476661.0004

in which our devices and algorithms have certain technical affordances and constraints that cause them to act much as literal filters do: straining out certain information and making other information more visible. We can think of our body and mind's ability to perceive certain things and not others as a set of cognitive filters. And we are part of cultures that also have their sets of filters: rituals, customs, terminologies, assumptions and prejudices that are sometimes visible to us and sometimes taken for granted.

DOI: 10.1057/9781137476661.0004

OPEN

3

Serial Selfies

Abstract: *Social media genres are cumulative and serial. Looking at an individual post, tweet, status update or selfie tells us only part of the story. To really understand social media genres we need to see them as feeds and analyse each post or image as a part of a series. This chapter looks at visual self-representational genres that are strongly serial: time-lapse selfie videos, profile photos in social media, and photobooths, one of the closest pre-digital precedents of today's selfies.*

Rettberg, Jill Walker. *Seeing Ourselves Through Technology: How We Use Selfies, Blogs and Wearable Devices to See and Shape Ourselves.* Basingstoke: Palgrave Macmillan, 2014. DOI: 10.1057/9781137476661.0005.

One Sunday in June of 2014 I wandered through the Elmhurst Art Gallery, a short drive outside of Chicago. Nadine Wasserman and Rachel Seligman had curated an exhibition they called 'LifeLoggers: Chronicling the Everyday'. The walls of one room were completely filled with hundreds of polaroids, many showing the face or body of artist Suzanne Szucs, who took photos every day over a period of 15 years and exhibits the photos in various configurations. Rather than curation, Szucs emphasises quantity and rhythm: a photograph every single day, no matter what. The immediacy of the photos is important, too: Szucs used an instant Polaroid camera and scribbled a few words or a sentence in the white space at the bottom of the photo.

The sheer mass of photographs in the gallery room was overwhelming. Some images were dull or silly: for several days Szucs only took photos of her own face with her tongue poking out. Others are very ordinary: friends having drinks together or a walk in the park. Some photos aim to break with conventional ideas of aesthetics and femininity in the visual, for instance showing Szucs in underpants with the sides of her sanitary napkin visibly sticking out. There are sequences that express great emotional pain after a breakup. An overexposed photo of her face, totally washed out, has the words 'BEYOND HOPE 4/5/05 1 am' written beneath it. The photos are organised in lines downwards, so the following day's photo is beneath this one, and shows a bleak three quarter profile shot of Szucs's face, slightly overexposed against a black background. A blurry selfie just beside it has the words 'Prewashed to limit shrinkage 4/5/05 5:27 pm'. Further over there are more selfies, with titles such as 'broken' (4/22), then shifting to metaphor with shots of her arm on two consecutive days ('The bruise takes on color 4/27/05 12pm' and 'Day 3 – not as bad as I thought 4/28/05 4:10 pm') and a little later, a photo of an empty, untidy bed, titled 'Unrest'.

Szucs's mass of self-portraits cannot be seen today without thinking of Instagram and the millions of selfies posted every day in social media. Szucs began her series in 1996, well before Instagram, but not before many people had begun sharing their lives online, in online diaries and on homepages. The Polaroid photos were already retro when Szucs used them: an analogue version of the filters offered today by Instagram and Hipstamatic.

Perhaps Szucs found the discipline of the daily Polaroid a useful way to keep making art in very small but very constant doses. Decades earlier, poet Frank O'Hara wrote autobiographical poems in his lunch

DOI: 10.1057/9781137476661.0005

breaks, enabling him, according to Todd Tietchen, 'to assert himself momentarily as the protagonist and author of his life events from within the persistent demands (or structuring proclivities) of technical time' (2014, 49). In Tietchen's comparison of O'Hara's poetry to 'situation-based microblogging' (51), he notes that O'Hara's lunch poems are in this respect not dissimilar to 'the 140 characters of the tweet that also make it possible to engage in self-authoring while frenetically involved in our quotidian demands' (49).

Cumulative self-presentations

Digital self-presentation and self-reflection is cumulative rather than presented as a definitive whole (J.W. Rettberg 2014, 5). A weblog or social media feed consists of a continuously expanded collection of posts, each of which may express a micro-narrative, a comment that expresses an aspect of the writer or an image showing a version of themselves. This cumulative logic is built into the software and into our habits of reading and sharing online, and it acts as a technological filter that lets certain kinds of content seep through while others are held back, either never being expressed or finding other outlets (see chapter 2). Szucs's series of Polaroids predates social media, though. She began the series when websites were eternally under construction and the structure of the digital was either hypertextual complexity or peer-to-peer chat spaces and listservs. And yet her project is so akin to today's streams of images, a little every day and the whole consists of nothing more than a potentially never-ending flow of fragments. Frank O'Hara's poems are even more clearly pre-digital. Yet Tietchen compares them to micro-blogging, as O'Hara escapes from the 'technical time' of a disciplined office worker's life to write a little each day. Of course it is easy to see the connections in hindsight, but Szucs and O'Hara also remind us that if the ways we structure our self-representations are technological filters built into our software and machines, they are *also* influenced by cultural filters.

Artists have anticipated almost every form of self-expression we see in digital media. Of course we not only have centuries of diaries and self-portraits, but also have flash narratives that are as short as tweets, photo-copied zines that episodically tell stories from the artist-author's life and artists, like Tehching Hsieh, who have taken photos of themselves every hour for a year.

DOI: 10.1057/9781137476661.0005

It is unlikely that the people who developed Twitter thought carefully about Frank O'Hara's poetry, or that Instagram's developers knew about the daily snapshots of artists like Szucs. Rather, both the artists and the developers create art and tools that respond to the culture at the time. The artists are usually first.

This chapter focuses on a selection of genres of serial visual self-representation online: time-lapse video self-portraits, profile pictures and self-improvement selfies. I also look at photobooths, which are an interesting historical precedent to today's selfies. All these forms emphasise the cumulative, serial practice that underlies most digital self-representations.

Time lapse selfies

On 11 August 2006, Ahree Lee uploaded a video of herself to YouTube. Four days later, 800,000 people had watched it (Washburn 2006). The video, titled *Me*, was a time-lapse video of photos Lee had taken of herself every day for three years. She began the project as a graduate student in graphic design and had exhibited it at several film festivals in 2003 and 2004, even winning awards, but posting it on YouTube gave it an entirely different kind of life as the start of a new genre. On 27 August 2006, Noah Kalina uploaded a very similar video to YouTube that he titled *Everyday*. He had also been taking daily photos of himself, for nearly six years, but only thought of making them into a video after seeing Lee's video *Me*. It was only a little over half a year since YouTube opened up to the public, and the site had skyrocketed in popularity. The web was ripe for viral videos. Kalina's video rapidly became even more popular than Lee's and quickly became the model for hundreds more videos in this genre.

If you use Google Trends to compare the interest in Lee's and Kalina's videos, you see that although Lee's video had a lot of interest just after she posted it, it was rapidly dwarfed by Kalina's video, which is still regularly searched for. Kalina has a Wikipedia page, Lee has none.

We might wonder why Kalina's video was much more successful than Lee's. The videos appear so similar: uploaded to YouTube in the same month by young people in their twenties who had taken daily photos while in art school or graphic design school. In both videos, the face of the artist is centred in the frame, and their faces are expressionless as backgrounds shift and change. Lee writes that she had made a similar video using photos of other people when she was in graduate school for graphic design, and she started the *Me* project wondering

DOI: 10.1057/9781137476661.0005

what such a video would look like if she was the only subject. Kalina had exhibited the photos at the School of Visual Arts in 2003, as a student, and it was seeing Lee's video that inspired him to make the photos into a video.

The current comments on Lee's video suggest that gender and race may have a lot to do with the different reception. There are slurs against Asians and against women ('now do it again with your tits'). Kalina doesn't escape YouTube comment fury, of course ('lol faggot boy what a loser you are noah') but most of the comments on his video are sympathetic. Although they both have expressionless faces, on Lee's video commenters assume she doesn't smile because she's Asian ('Lol she's asian so she looked the same for the whole thing') whereas commenters on Kalina's video ask him 'y so sad' with concern or simply comment 'Poker face.'

Kalina and Lee are of course not the first people to have taken daily photos of themselves. Szucs's daily photographs are one example, but even in the genre of daily headshots there are precedents. Photographer Karl Baden (2007) has taken daily photos every day since 1987 and has exhibited the photos at several places. He now shares them on a blog he keeps for the project. Baden's face has the same lack of expression as in Lee's and Kalina's photos, but where Lee and Kalina shoot the photos in their homes, with various, often messy, backgrounds, Baden always poses in front of a white wall. His photos are all framed identically so that only the head and torso is visible. The shoulders are bare, so while we saw Lee's and Kalina's clothes change with each image, Baden looks the same: clean and contextless except for his hair and the date scrawled at the bottom of the image. His photographs are black and white in a portrait format and apart from the naked shoulders look just like identity card photographs.

No doubt many other artists and photographers have taken daily photos of themselves. I mentioned Eleanor Antin's *Carving*, from 1972, in chapter 1. Antin took 4 photos of herself a day for 37 days while on a diet: one photo showing her body from the front, one from the back and one from each side. The photos show her full, standing body, and her face is expressionless. Antin lost 10 pounds during the 37 days the project lasted, metaphorically carving fat off her own body, but the weight loss can barely even be seen in the photographs.

An important work in the history of serial visual self-representations is Tehching Hsieh's *One Year Performance 1980–81*, also known as the 'Time

DOI: 10.1057/9781137476661.0005

Clock Piece'. Hsieh punched a time clock in his studio every hour for a full year, and each time he also took his photograph (Miall 2014). The self-portraits were taken on 16mm film, one photograph on each frame of the film strip, so at the end of the year, he had a six minute movie of his face. At the start of the year Hsieh shaved his head, so watching his hair grow as the year progresses is the clearest indication of the passing of time. He always wears the same grey uniform, with his name embroidered on the pocket, clearly referencing the relentless time tracking of the factory worker.

After Lee's and especially Kalina's videos went viral, hundreds if not thousands of similar videos have been posted online, and many of these have become very popular too. People use daily photographs of their own faces, their pregnant bellies or their children to create personal time-lapse videos, and many very clearly reference Kalina's work in particular, for instance by using the same music as he used in their videos. It has become technically trivial to create videos like this. As if digital cameras and home video editing software wasn't enough, websites were quickly dedicated to making it even easier to work in the genre. Dailymugshot. com has apps for your phone to make your time-lapse selfie video even easier to create. Dailybooth.com shut down in 2012, but previously would generate animated sequences from your daily webcam selfies that used the music composed for Kalina's video *Everyday*. Now we use smartphones more often than webcams for our selfies, and there are apps such as Everyday, Selfie Time Lapse Camera and Picr that will remind you to take your daily photo, help you line up your camera so your face is positioned the same in each image, and automatically generate a video of your daily selfies.

Part of the fascination of watching time lapse selfies is watching how the subject changes and eventually ages. In the section about *Me* on her website, Lee compares her video to 'the vanitas tradition of still life painting', writing that 'the ephemerality of physical appearance and the inevitability of aging and mortality' is implicit in the work. Elizabeth Losh notes that Lee's and Kalina's videos are strangely lacking in affect. Their faces are expressionless, the only things that change are hair, clothes and the slow process of aging (Losh 2014). Perhaps this is in reference to earlier artists: Antin and Hsieh don't smile. Neither does Baden. Or perhaps they are attempting, impossibly, to remain constant with the world around us and even our own faces change with the passing of time.

DOI: 10.1057/9781137476661.0005

Not all time-lapse selfies are devoid of smiles and emotion. A moving example is Rebecca Brown's video of photos she took of herself every day from 2007 when she was 14 until 2014, when she was 21. At first she smiles. Her expression changes often, her hair is long and worn in many different fashions and the backgrounds and lighting constantly change. Sometimes there are other people with her in the selfies. She is playful. She holds a hand in front of her eyes in one image and has drawn a moustache on her lip in another. As the years go by, though, her smiles give way to a standard expression: a faint smile that sometimes but not always seems to extend to her eyes. Hair growth and hair cuts are always important in time lapse selfies, but in Brown's case hair is particularly important: she explains that she has trichotillomania, a condition which caused her to lose her hair and cut it short at many points.

Unlike Kalina's and Lee's videos, Brown's video is annotated with short text fragments in the black side bars. We see the years flick by: '2009. 2010. 2011.' Explanatory notes pop up and disappear in turn: 'Diagnosed with depression. Severely Depressed Suicidal. Recovered and Passed A levels. New York 2011! Went to University. Art/Film.' The apparent honesty in these written notes contrasts with the constant slight smile she wears. She looks OK. She looks happier than Kalina and Lee, but far less happy than her 14-year-old self at the start of the movie. At the end of the movie Brown shows an image from each year, moving back-wards to the happy 14-year-old. Then she appears in the frame as the young adult she currently is, bright and cheerful with beautiful hair and makeup, in standard video rather than time-lapse animation, and speaks directly to us, inviting us to follow her YouTube channel (click here) or to learn more about trichotillomania (click there). Brown clearly has a purpose with her video. She deliberately uses her self-portrait to break down taboos about depression and mental health, showing her difficult times but also reassuring us that she's doing better now. She includes a FAQ in the info box for the video on YouTube. One of the questions is as follows: 'Q: Where does the smile go? A: Life happens, Depression hit rather hard. I'm on the mend.'

Brown's video is far more playful and, at the start, more cheerful than Lee's, Kalina's or Baden's projects were. Looking at the many time lapse videos parents make of their children growing from babies to teenagers we see the same joy and affect. Search for 'Natalie Time Lapse: Birth to 10 years old in 1 minute 25 sec' (viewed more than eight million times) or another video of a child growing up on YouTube, and you'll see laugh-

DOI: 10.1057/9781137476661.0005

ing, smiling children. Their eyes may be centred in the frame as Lee's and Kalina's were, but these children's hands and mouths move, making it appear that they are eagerly telling us all about their lives.

Clearly the work of artists such as Antin, Hsieh and others anticipates today's selfies. But most people who create selfies today are not aware of these forebears. They may have seen Kalina's and perhaps Lee's videos and have certainly seen videos by others who themselves were inspired by Kalina and Lee. As selfies increasingly become part of our vernacular culture, it is likely that more of us will generate our own time lapse videos in some way or another. At the end of 2013, Facebook generated personalised videos for each user, consisting of photos from their timelines. Perhaps next year we will have posted enough selfies that the annual video will be an automatically generated time lapse video of our own faces.

Profile photos as visual identity

Not everyone takes or shares selfies, but most of us have accounts on Facebook or other social media. One of the first things you are asked to do when you create a social media account is to upload a profile photo. We often use photographs taken of us by other people for our profile pictures, so they are not always selfies, but a profile picture is a visual expression of identity, and our choice of profile photos is clearly a form of visual self-representation. Similar to selfies taken for time lapse videos, profile pictures change over time. Some of us barely ever update them, while others upload a new one every couple of weeks. Like most self-representations in digital media, profile photos are part of a serial and cumulative visual communication.

Profile pictures don't always show a person's face. Sometimes the profile picture marks not individual identity but a connection to a social group or political cause. These can be frivolous, like the little Santa hats various apps can automatically add to your Facebook or Twitter profile photo, or they can be deeply serious. In a study of the Kurdish diaspora's use of social media, Kurdin Jacob describes how her informants post photos of themselves wearing Kurdish clothes and with the Kurdish flag to display their Kurdish identity. Kurdistan is not officially recognised as a nation, but millions of Kurdish people living abroad use photos such as these as a way to show their pride in being a Kurd, to strengthen their shared

DOI: 10.1057/9781137476661.0005

identity with other Kurds in diaspora and as a challenge to Facebook's rule against posting images of the Kurdish flag (Jacob 2013, 65–8).

Icons can be added and removed from profile pictures to mark seasons or events. People add Santa hats for Christmas and flags to show support for their team or country during sports events or for political reasons. Icons or flags are also often used as temporary profile pictures instead of the standard photo of the user's face. After the bomb in Oslo and the massacre on Utøya in 2011, many Norwegians used the OSLOVE icon or a rose instead of their profile image. Another way of using the profile image as an identity marker is by using a photo showing the profile holder with a friend, a child, a lover or a group of friends (Mendelson and Papacharissi 2011). Some users even use a photo of themselves as a child, or a photo of their own child instead of a photo of themselves, in a move that simultaneously anonymises them a little and shows how profile pictures can function as metonyms: this is part of me. Profile photos can change frequently, as new selfies they like, as they use the [changing profile pictures] or a political cause or a group, or as they want new representations of themselves.

In an article about Tanzanian students' Facebook profile photos, Paula Uimonen (2013) describes such changing self-representations and how they connect the individual to national and global identities. One of the young women she interviewed used a photo of herself lying smiling in autumn leaves after an exchange year in the UK, clearly showing that she was in a place with a different climate than Tanzania. A while later, she switched to a Tanzanian flag, leaving out her face altogether. Another of Uimonen's informants used a portrait image where the colours of the Tanzanian flag were overlaid on an image of his face, and at another point, an image of his face superimposed on a map of Africa with the words 'Strictly African'.

These kinds of visual identity performance in social media can also be coercive; people can feel pressured into demonstrating a certain group identity. In her recent book *It's Complicated* (2014), danah boyd writes about a young African American from South Central Los Angeles who wrote a college application letter about how he longed to get away from the gangs in his neighbourhood, but had a Myspace account filled with gang-related imagery. The college admissions office contacted boyd, assuming that the Myspace account represented the young man's true identity and asking why he would lie in his admission essay when it was

DOI: 10.1057/9781137476661.0005

so easy to find his 'true' self online. It's not that simple, boyd argues in her book, writing that he probably felt that not to show membership in a gang would be outright dangerous:

> Without knowing the teen, my guess was that he was genuine in his college essay. At the same time, I also suspected that he would never dare talk about his desire to go to a prestigious institution in his neighborhood because doing so would cause him to be ostracized socially, if not physically attacked. (boyd 2014, 30)

In a sense we present a different version of ourselves in each profile picture we choose. In social media we not only present different fronts to different groups of people, as Goffman described in his foundational work on self-presentation (Goffman 1959; Markham 2013a), but we also change our self-presentation over time.

Automatic portraits

Photobooth photos are one of the closest relatives of today's selfies, with their almost-instant production of photographs, the mirror in the booth and resulting photos that often look very similar to today's digital selfies. Although forerunners to the fully automatic photo booths were seen as early as the 1890s (Pellicer 2010, 16), the photobooth was patented in 1925 by Anatol Josepho, and rapidly became a popular attraction in fairs, amusement parks and department stores. As Raynal Pellicer writes in his well-illustrated history of photobooths, fun was emphasised in the advertising of this new technology: having your picture taken was 'no longer a chore – now it's a game', the ads proclaimed.

The surrealists saw the photobooth as a perfect complement to their artistic program. In the first surrealist manifesto, published in 1924, André Breton famously defined surrealism as 'psychic automatism in its pure state, by which one proposes to express, either verbally, or in writing, or in any other manner, the actual functioning of thought' (1969, 26). Automated self-portraits were a perfect surrealist method, and many self-portraits taken by the surrealists have been preserved. As can be seen in the examples displayed in Pellicer's book *Photobooth* (2010), or on the many Pinterest boards and blogs that host photos of surrealist photobooth self-portraits, the surrealists behaved very similarly to us when they found a machine that would let them take photos of themselves. There are goofy faces, questioning gazes and grimaces.

DOI: 10.1057/9781137476661.0005

But even at this point, surrealists saw the photobooth as a tool for self-exploration. Look at this definition of 'photomaton' written by a group of surrealists for the 15 December 1928 issue of *Variétés: revue menuelle illustrée de l'esprit contemporain*:

> The Photomaton is an automatic device that provides you, in exchange for a five-france token, with a strip of eight attitudes caught in photographs. Photomaton, I've been seen, you've seen me, I've often seen myself. There are fanatics who collect hundreds of their 'expressions'. It is a system of psychoanalysis via image. The first strip surprises you as you struggle to find the individual you always believed yourself to be. After the second strip, and throughout all the many strips that follow, while you may do your best to play the superior individual, the original type, the dark fascinating one, or the monkey, none of the resulting visions will fully correspond to what you want to see in yourself. (qtd by Pellicer 2010, 92)

This testing out of different possible variations of the self is very much present in today's digital selfies as well. Perhaps the reason we feel the need to take another, and yet another selfie, is in part that we as the surrealists wrote in the 1928 never seem able to create a photo that will 'fully correspond to what you want to see in yourself.'

The automation of the photobooth is obviously closely connected to today's selfies, although a selfie with a digital camera allows the photographer far more freedom and aesthetic options than did the photobooth. The analogue, physical photobooth both gave and refused to give the subject control over their own image. As Priscilla Frank (2012) writes, commenting on an exhibition of photobooth art at the Musée d'Elysée in Lausanne in 2012,

> it makes sense that surrealists would be entranced by the photo booth, an automaton that operated independently of human consciousness or human hands. Even the subjects were barely in control of their position, those photo flashes come too fast. The resulting images are pure, independent imaging; the subject is caught in limbo between pose and natural stance. In the endless stream of images, strip after strip, the people themselves lose their humanity and begin to look like automatic images as well.

Of course, although the surrealists and many artists since have used the photobooth for art, the most frequent use of the photobooth was by non-artists, playing around, documenting a special event or a friendship or relationship or simply taking identity photos.

DOI: 10.1057/9781137476661.0005

When you stepped into a photobooth you would draw a curtain to hide yourself from the world. The curious combination of intimate, hidden space within a public setting (often there would be a line of people right outside the curtain, waiting to use the photo booth after you were done) is an interesting counterpoint to the line between public and private we see in today's selfies: the moment of photography is intimate. There is nothing there but the person herself and the machine, the camera. There is no other human to operate the camera or to tell you how to pose or to make you embarrassed – unless the photograph is of several people, which was often the case in a photobooth as it is in today's selfies.

There are Pinterest boards and blogs that collect photobooth photographs of celebrities long gone. Search for some and look at the uncertain gaze of Elvis Presley, Audrey Hepburn, Marguerite Duras and other faces we know better from professional portraits. Elvis seems to be practicing the smouldering gaze he later perfects. Duras looks seriously into her own reflected eyes, as we all do in the mirror. These imperfect, unpolished photos have a sense of introspection that humanises them and reminds us of our own time's selfies.

The serial nature of most digital self-representation is closely connected to the tradition of the diary, which is written bit by bit over a period of time. It is also connected to pre-digital quantitative self-representations, where data is likewise collected and logged over time. In the next chapter, we look at automated diaries that combine the serial with the apparent objectivity of an external device quantitatively measuring our behaviours.

DOI: 10.1057/9781137476661.0005

OPEN

4

Automated Diaries

Abstract: *Today's diary writes itself for you. Apps can turn your smartphone into an automated diary that will keep track of where you go, sort your photos for you and pull in your social media updates to generate detailed records of your life. Lifelogging cameras like the Narrative Clip are clipped to your shirt and automatically take a photo every 30 seconds throughout the day. This chapter discusses the information and images that these devices record and the ways in which they present the data to try to make it meaningful for the user. Are our devices 'active cognizers', to use N. Katherine Hayles' term, making us cyborg selves collaborating with our machines? How do these devices and apps filter our lives?*

Rettberg, Jill Walker. *Seeing Ourselves Through Technology: How We Use Selfies, Blogs and Wearable Devices to See and Shape Ourselves.* Basingstoke: Palgrave Macmillan, 2014. DOI: 10.1057/9781137476661.0006.

Diaries are always, in a sense, written in real time. As engaged readers or followers of online self-representations, we always crave the next post, the next image, the next bit of the story. The very act of starting a blog or an Instagram or Facebook account carries with it an intention to write or share more, again, another day. As Phillippe Lejeune writes of diaries, 'All journal writing assumes the intention to write at least one more time, an entry that will call for yet another one, and so on without end. ... To "finish" a diary means to cut it off from the future' (2001, 100–1). Social media embed this 'call for yet another one' into the software. Facebook asks 'What's on your mind?', Twitter offers me retweet buttons and a box to write my tweets in, and HeyDay and OptimizeMe push notifications to the home screen of my phone, suggesting I might want to look at my photos or update the log of my activities today.

The ultimate real-time diary is a diary that writes itself automatically, without needing your input. Smartphones are ideal devices for logging our day-to-day experiences. For a start, they automatically store information about what we are doing: a phone can log our geographic location and thus where we go and how fast we are moving from place to place, and many models can also track motions, meaning it can estimate whether we are running, climbing or dancing. Some phones sense far more than this. The 'Sensors Overview' on Android.com's pages for developers explains how to use data from platforms that have sensors for temperature, light, pressure, humidity, gravity and more. The phone not only knows whether we make phone calls or send texts or emails, but also knows which apps we use and what we search for online. It knows what version of the operating system we are using, what music we play, what videos we watch and what we read. It can measure how fast we read and the style of our writing. In the final chapter of this book, I discuss the implications of our devices' automatic tracking for privacy and surveillance, but in this chapter I explore how we are beginning to use this automatic tracking to document and explore our own lives.

We are currently seeing more and more examples of continuous, automated, real-time diaries, where our everyday use of technology is converted into a journal-like format. Location sharing was one of the first aspects of personal data to be automatically logged at the user's request, first with services such as Plazes.com, which logged you as being at a new location every time it saw that your laptop was connected from a different IP number (J.W. Rettberg 2014, 86), and later with smartphone apps such as Foursquare and Swarm that use the phone's built in GPS and

DOI: 10.1057/9781137476661.0006

other location tracking systems to allow the user to check in at different locations. These services generate a chronological list of places that the user was at, and award 'badges' or similar rewards or markers showing the kinds of places users spend a lot of time at. Foursquare's badges have titles such as Jetsetter (airports), Mall Rat (shopping malls), Trainspotter (train stations), Baker's Dozen (bakeries) and Great Outdoors (parks and nature areas). Some of the badges are more interpretative: School Night is awarded for checking in after 3 am on a school night, and 9 to 5 is for checking in at work 15 times in 30 days.

Newer services make location-based diaries even more seamless. Why wait to check in or manually post a photo or text when the technology I carry with me can automatically track where I am and organise all my photos and texts for me? Sites such as TimeHop allow us to connect our various social media streams and add in text messages and photos sent or taken on our phones to create a timeline of our days. More recently, automatic journaling apps for our phones such as HeyDay, Saga, Chronos or Step combine information about our movements using GPS, the photos we take and connected services like Facebook, TripIt, Runkeeper and more to create automatically organised diaries of our days with little or no direct input from us.

Life poetry told by sensors

The marketing for the many lifelogging apps that are available by mid-2014 tells us of a vision of authentic, meaningful diaries created by machines for people. Saga's slogan is 'Choose your own adventure,' and their website continues: 'Be bold. Embrace your authentic self. Record your life automatically and share it effortlessly with the people you care about' (2014). STEP journal's iTunes App Store pitch is even more enthusiastic: 'STEP Journal assists you in capturing and telling the amazing story of your life. Life poetry told by sensors – minimal efforts and 100% privacy. The true power of Automatic Journaling!' Their website proclaims 'Moments turned into meaning,' and continues, 'Want to know yourself better? STEP Journal makes it easy to collect your life moments and manage them using quantified and visualized dashboard. It's a beautiful way to enrich your life' (2014). Friday is another lifelogging app. It not only tracks what you do, but also tries to predict what you'll want to do. The description for the app in Google Play assures potential users

DOI: 10.1057/9781137476661.0006

that 'Friday initiates thoughts and ideas for you, it helps you remember, it tries to anticipate actions' (2014). Chronos Data Collector and OptimizeMe also try to help you analyse and improve your life by automatically logging it. On the Chronos website, we read 'Find your time. See how you are spending your time without lifting a finger. Chronos runs in the background on your phone and automatically captures every moment' (2014). The blurb for OptimizeMe reads 'Get the best out of every day of your life. Simply track your everyday life with OptimizeMe and learn how to improve it' (2014).

Several of these apps emphasise the *story* they promise to tell of your life in their very names: Saga, Narrato, Storica and Evertale are examples. They promise to analyse your daily movements and actions and to create meaning, help you get to know yourself better, get the best out of every day, enrich your life, improve your life – and predict what you might be interested in doing next.

I installed several of the apps on my phone and let them track me for a few weeks, curious to see how they would represent my life. OptimizeMe was not automatic at all, and it required me to spend time every day entering my activities, my energy level, productivity and mood for each entry. After two weeks it began to show me 'correlations', but they were not very useful. For instance, on days when I slept less, I tended to log my writing as being more productive – perhaps because I wrote less and slept more on weekends. Saga tracked my movements automatically and connected to Facebook, Runkeeper, Twitter and various other apps to generate an automatic log of my life, but I had to correct its guesses about where I was, and its promised helpful information that would be relevant to my individual life mostly consisted of repeated notifications about concerts at the local grocery store. I had one happy moment with Saga's personalised information the day after I installed it. When I was exploring the hedge maze at the Morton Arboretum outside Chicago with my family, Saga beeped my phone to warn me that it was going to start raining in nine minutes. Sure enough, a heavy but brief downpour began soon after, and I was grateful we had time to find shelter. Of course, other weather apps will do the same thing only using my location. Saga didn't need to know my whole life to warn me of rain.

Chronos worked similarly to Saga, but without the connections to other social media services, and sent me weekly infographic reports on my life, which quite appealed to me. Back in 2008, I was intrigued when the now defunct travel site Dopplr sent me a similar personalised graph

DOI: 10.1057/9781137476661.0006

(J.W. Rettberg 2009) and the graphs Chronos sends are clear descendants. The level of detail is astounding, though not always correct. For instance, the infographic shows the average hours and minutes I sleep on weekdays and weekends, basing my bedtime on when I turn my phone face down and leave it alone for a few hours and wake up time on when the phone is moved again. It estimates my time working based on how much time I spend at places I have categorised as 'work'. It gives me a score for how social I am based on how much time I spend at places that are categorised as social/out, such as cafés, restaurants, movie theatres and museums. There are also some very normative scores. For instance, I scored 100% for work-life balance on the week I was on a family vacation and spent no time at places categorised as 'work', and 73% for spontaneity the same week, presumably because I didn't do the same things as I do most weeks. Chronos also tracks time spent with my friends, but only friends who have also installed Chronos, and I don't have many of them. I imagine the developers who made this app creating these measures of their imagined perfect persona, and think of Alice Marwick's (2013) descriptions of the ways in which the ideologies and culture of Silicon Valley developers have permeated social media, inscribing quite specific cultural values into the tools that are used by billions around the world. But in addition to these cultural filters that are built into the app, the app is of course also constrained by technological filters: an iPhone can easily track a user's location, or whether the phone is face down and still or not, but it can't really know whether a user is working or sleeping. These apps can see that I'm 'in transit' when I do the child drop off and pickup rounds every morning and afternoon, but none of them register that the five minutes I spend at each of their schools are in fact fairly important points in my day. I don't spend long enough there for the locations to even show up in my logs.

Capture All

A couple of weeks before I finished this book, the call for works for the upcoming 2015 Transmediale arts festival was published. 'CAPTURE ALL,' the website proclaims: 'Track steps. Track sleep. Track habits. Get fit. Get better. Update status. Count Heartbeats. Like Friends. Reach your goals. Share. Be influential. Be original. Find backers and back others. Work more. Work less. Be mindful. Send rewards. Predict actions. Chal-

DOI: 10.1057/9781137476661.0006

lenge yourself. Become a Low-Carb Data Hero. Play the game. Track life.'
The festival will showcase works that 'outsmart and outplay the logic of
CAPTURE ALL and that organise more intimate modes of post-digital
life, work and play,... operating in and exploiting the blind spots of a
datafied society.'

Transmediale is responding to the logic of a culture where it has
become possible to record everything. We can store all our photographs,
all our emails and all our text messages. Leaving the personal we also
know that Google is trying to digitise all books ever published, that they
are pretty close to having indexed all webpages and that they store data
about all searches. This is very useful to us. I love being able to use Google
Book search to search through old print books, or Google Trends to look
at what people searched for in 2006, but it is a huge cultural shift from a
very recent time where we had to select what to record, what to save and
what to forget or discard.

The urge to exhaustively document everything is not new. In the
late 1940s, the psychologist Roger Barker led a project attempting to
document every moment of ordinary peoples' lives, as a counter to the
constructed laboratory experiments that dominated psychology research
at the time. Roger Barker and Herbert Wright's book *One Boy's Day* (1951)
is a 435 page record of everything that happens to a seven-year-old boy
during one fourteen hour day, recorded minute by minute by a team of
eight observers. While the book was criticised for its lack of analysis or
theory, being nothing but raw data, Barker later published an anthology
of studies based on such 'behavior streams' as he called them (Barker
1963), coining a term very reminiscent of the streams and feeds of data
we create and read today. And yet, even as videotaping made recording
simpler, this kind of intense collection of every detail of a person's life
did not become a common methodology until in the last few years, as
computers have made it feasible not only to store such detailed logs but
also to automatically record the data in the first place and to manipulate
and analyse it. The Quantified Self movement with its blogs, conferences
and meetups is the personal equivalent to big data: collecting and analysing data about oneself. Barker would have been thrilled to see the detailed
streams of information about human behaviour collected by quantified
selfers. But despite the promise of 'big data' we are still working out what
kinds of questions can be answered by the data. Perhaps, as Alessandro
Marcengo and Amon Rapp argue, echoing the critics of Barker's work
half a century ago, Quantified Self 'is not something oriented to build

DOI: 10.1057/9781137476661.0006

knowledge toward a purpose, but instead a way to collect data, like collecting butterflies [or] beer caps. [It is an] end in itself' (2014, 240). Perhaps we simply want to 'capture all'.

A photo every 30 seconds

The urge to gather and to collect is ancient among humans. Until recently, we have not attempted to 'capture all'. Collections have usually required some form of selection and curation. When we make photo albums or write diaries or post a photo to Instagram we intentionally choose what we want to remember and share and what we want to leave out. What happens when we automate the process? What happens when we try to capture everything?

The Narrative Clip is one of the first consumer products that promises to visually capture all of your life. The website explains, 'The Narrative Clip is a tiny, automatic camera and app that gives you a searchable and shareable photographic memory.' You clip the camera onto your clothing and it takes a photo every 30 seconds. 'Remember every moment,' the website urges as of 28 May 2014:

> Capture the moment as it happens, without interference. Complement your staged photos of majestic scenery with the intensity of the small moments that matter the most.

The Narrative Clip is a descendent of custom built wearable cameras such as those pioneered by Steve Mann. His earliest head-mounted cameras were developed in the late 1970s, and he has continued developing them ever since, wearing them every day. Mann's systems aren't primarily intended for self-representation: rather, they provide the user with extra information about the world around them. In the mid-nineties Mann streamed continuous video from the camera he wore to his website, which became very popular. Soon thereafter, webcams became cheap enough to be a reasonable addition to a home computer, and video streaming from home became fairly common. Jennifer Ringley's JenniCam went live in 1996, broadcasting to the internet from her dorm room, in the vanguard of a whole genre of 'camgirls'. As quoted in Theresa Senft's *Camgirls: Celebrity and Community in the Age of Social Networks* (2008), Ringley wanted 'to show people that what we see on TV—people with perfect hair, perfect friends, perfect lives—is not reality. I'm reality' (16).

DOI: 10.1057/9781137476661.0006

The aesthetic of the everyday and the ordinary and what Ellen Rutten (2014) calls the aesthetics of imperfection is familiar to us from reality television, craft blogs and oddly-cropped Instagram photos. Awkward angles, poor focus and unharmonious composition are all markers of a certain kind of visual realism. The automatic snapshots generated by the Narrative clip certainly fall within this aesthetic.

The first day I wore my Narrative Clip I fastened it to my shirt at chest height. Downloading the images at the end of the day, I found dozens of photos of trees and clouds, some obscured by my long hair partially covering the camera. The camera had been tilted upwards due to the angle of my breasts. Looking at the Wikipedia entry for 'Lifelogging' I noticed a composite image of four phases of wearable camera from Steve Mann in the 1980s until today, where the cameras were all worn on necklaces, by flat chested men in t-shirts. Lifelogging cameras were designed for people with flat chests, I concluded.

So I tried wearing the camera higher, clipping it to the top of my shirt's neckline, almost up by my shoulder, hoping that this would tilt it to capture more of what I saw when looking straight ahead. The results weren't much better, but the device did capture some faces of passersby in addition to the clouds and trees. I wore it walking to my six-year-old's school to pick her up and walking home with her as she cheerfully rode her scooter beside me. To my disappointment, when I viewed the images, my daughter was not in any of the photos. Neither did the Narrative Clip capture any photos of my four-year-old son when I wore the camera while playing with him at a playground. My children were invisible to the camera. I tried wearing it clipped to the pocket of my jeans instead, thinking I just needed to get the camera closer to their height. This time it did capture a couple of blurry photographs of the backs of my kids' heads as they shot off ahead of me on their scooters. But the photos from the playground itself were mostly of the clouds again, because when I sat down to watch the kids play the camera, still fastened to the front pocket of my jeans, tilted upwards. After the playground we went to a café, and there the camera captured its hitherto clearest images of people. Unfortunately, the people captured were the people at the table next to ours, people I had barely noticed at the time. The next day, I walked with my daughter again, and we sat down to eat our lunch, happening to sit across from a large advertisement pasted to the brick wall. My Narrative Clip captured several photos of the model's face, and its facial recognition algorithms marked this as an important moment, making the ad

DOI: 10.1057/9781137476661.0006

the cover image for the series of photos from that afternoon. Later, my daughter wore the camera during her ballet class. Even there, with mirrors covering the walls and the camera clipped to the chest of her leotard, at the same height as the other children, almost all the images were of the ceiling, or her long hair falling in front of the lens, or the back of another child's head.

Clearly, the Narrative Clip doesn't record my subjectively memorable moments. It doesn't even record what I see: in fact, the 'best' images – such as those of the people at the table next to ours at the café or the photo of the advertisement pasted on the wall – are photos of people and things that were outside of my field of vision or that I had quickly dismissed as unimportant. Strikingly, my children were almost completely erased from my life as envisioned by the Narrative Clip. That is certainly not the intention of the camera. On the contrary, their marketing videos show parents capturing everyday moments with children.

The Narrative Clip photographs indiscriminately. A photo is taken every 30 seconds no matter what is in the frame. Back when we had to buy film for our cameras and pay to have it developed, we had to think about the expense of each photograph we chose to take. The cost wasn't simply financial, we also had to consider how many shots were left on the roll of film, as we wouldn't want to run out of film before we had captured a range of interesting images. With digital photography, individual photos have no cost, unless we are close to running out of battery or memory space. A camera that takes photos regardless of whether there is anything worth photographing is a natural development.

Digital photography also changes what is *photographable*, to use a term from Pierre Bourdieu's book *Photography: A Middle-Brow Art*. The book was first published in French in 1960, a time when photography was already a very common everyday practice. Bourdieu argued that what is photographable, seen as worthy of being photographed, is quite rigidly determined by social norms. Perhaps much of the discomfort we see surfacing around selfies is related to this: we are still bound by these social norms but technology allows us to photograph so much more than when the social norms for photography developed. The technological filter has changed, but the cultural filters are still in the process of changing.

Bourdieu doesn't directly write about self-portraits, but he does note that posture in photographs is important. He writes that '[t]o strike a pose is to offer oneself to be captured in a posture which is not and which

DOI: 10.1057/9781137476661.0006

does not seek to be "natural" (1990, 80). Photography, for most people, was a ritual. It was not something done every day or continuously, but something that marked important events. On the other end of the scale, the marketing for the Narrative Clip claims that the most important events to capture for the future are not necessarily birthdays and weddings, but moments that are not usually photographed. Photography is no longer about documenting social rituals, but about documenting the everyday.

Clearly, part of the reason we take more photos is that technology makes it possible, easy and cheap. This is the technological filter that gives us the aesthetics of the everyday. If we always have a camera in our pockets, of course we will take more photos, and many of those photos will be taken on days when there are no ritual events happening: no weddings, birthdays or funerals. There is also a cultural filter, perhaps originating in reality television, but also strengthened by seeing more of each other's photos on Instagram and in blogs. Even studio photography shows this shift. In her study of a photography studio run by three consecutive generations of a family in a small Norwegian town, Sigrid Lien (2014) shows that it is not just the photographer's aesthetics of wedding photography that have changed from the 1960s until today. The most recent photographs are heavily influenced by the portrait subjects' own familiarity with photography and the digital, and include many informal shots. Often the bride and groom's faces aren't even clearly visible. In one of the photos Lien discusses in her article, the groom faces away from the viewer as he holds his bride's hand, leading her away from us into a field of daisies as she smiles back at the camera. In another the couple are seated in a boat on water, but their faces are outside of the frame.

There are also technological reasons for the new emphasis on capturing everyday moments rather than established rituals, as there were for the more rigid style of older photos. The photography studio studied by Lien is currently run by a young woman who has taken over from her father as he once took over from his father. The woman's father told Lien about accompanying his father on photo shoots in the sixties: 'Back then everything was much more uncertain and straining, ... particularly when you came back and were about to develop the films. Consequently you were more bound up and had to run the whole thing very safely' (147). The granddaughter, the photographer who takes the contemporary wedding photos, explains that today they think about series of

DOI: 10.1057/9781137476661.0006

photographs instead of single images: 'We can tell a story. I think album. I think presentation' (148). The serial nature of digital images, that I discussed in chapter 3, spills over into studio photography as well. The technology comes with certain constraints and affordances, but cultural filters are also crucial.

Algorithms to find meaning

The Narrative Clip is marketed not as a stream to the public, but as a private record of your days. The vast quantities of data need to be analysed if they are to be useful as a diary. The iPhone app where users can browse through their photos needs to analyse the images to display them in meaningful groups, based for example on location or people in the images, and to emphasise the most important images. Here every moment of a day is recorded as potential material for a diary, and only afterwards is it edited. Of course, the algorithms that determine what is displayed as important are written by people who decide on how to make the selection based on both our cultural filters and on what is possible or easy to do given the affordances and constraints of our technology.

For instance, what can biometric software analysis 'see' in images? It can recognise faces, and we might assume that an image with a face in it is more important than an image of an empty field, but the software cannot know if that field is in fact meaningful to the person who saw it. Perhaps you are standing staring at a now serene WWII battlefield where your grandfather was killed. Perhaps the poppies growing there are extremely meaningful to you, but how would the software know that? The camera can automatically collect visual information but lacks the knowledge of the human's emotions and memories that make those images meaningful or not.

Biometric or other algorithmic visual analysis may be able to recognise what Roland Barthes calls the *studium*, the average affect a person feels about most photos, where he or she may be interested in the literal content of the photograph or about what it says about a place or a period (1981, 26). But algorithms cannot yet find Barthes' *punctum*, the 'wound' that makes a photograph poignant to an individual. The punctum is not generalisable (27). A photo that affects me strongly (a three second video my uncle sent me showing my grandmother in profile, the light of the setting sun soft upon her wrinkled skin, a gentle smile in her eyes as she

DOI: 10.1057/9781137476661.0006

nods, showing her as I remember her as a child) will mean nothing to you. For me there is a *punctum*, for you, perhaps you are interested in the image as a *studium* or perhaps not at all. Barthes' description of the way he experiences the *studium* reminds me of the way a machine reads an image:

> [T]he photograph can 'shout,' not wound. These journalistic photographs are received (all at once), perceived. I glance through them, I don't recall them; no detail (in some corner) ever interrupts my reading: I am interested in them (as I am interested in the world), I do not love them. (41)

And yet, sometimes, the renditions of our days that a device such as the Narrative Clip might provide, or the automated videos of our year that Facebook generated at the end of 2013, do show us ourselves in ways that we find meaningful. Many friends I ask tell me that they hated Facebook's end-of-year video of their life, but there are also a fair share who liked them and thought they were a meaningful representation of some aspect of their life, perhaps even finding a *punctum* where others found none. We can imagine software that would learn what particularly moved each user. Maybe the software would register that a particular Narrative Clip user tended to pause and spend time near flowers, or trains, and might surmise that flowers, or trains, were particularly meaningful to that user. With this knowledge, the software might then further emphasise those items when displaying the user's photos, approaching what N. Katherine Hayles writes of when describing the machine as an active cognizer (2004, 84). Facebook, Google and other services constantly tweak their attempts to give us personally meaningful news feeds and search results based on our individual previous interactions, searches and likes (Bucher 2012) as well as on the words we use and many other factors (Kramer, Guillory and Hancock 2014; Gillespie 2014).

When our computers write our diaries for us, automatically logging where we've been, who we've communicated with, how we moved, what we ate and what photos we took, we have allowed technology to become very deeply enmeshed in our self-representations. Even when we write a diary in a blank paper book we are enmeshed in technology, bound by its constraints and affordances (Kirschenbaum 2012), but these automatic journaling apps do more than that, they are what Hayles calls *active cognizers*. She writes about the differences between print literature and electronic literature such as hypertext fictions or kinetic poetry, but if anything the computational processes involved in logging, analysing

DOI: 10.1057/9781137476661.0006

and presenting our lives in the apps discussed in this chapter are even more involved in the distributed cognition Hayles describes:

> It is no longer a question of whether computers are intelligent. Any cognizer that can perform the acts of evaluation, judgment, synthesis, and analysis exhibited by expert systems and autonomous agent software programs should prima facie be considered intelligent. ... When we read electronic hypertexts, we do so in environments that include the computer as an active cognizer performing sophisticated acts of interpretation and representation. Thus cognition is distributed not only between writer, reader, and designer (who may or may not be separate people) but also between humans and machines (which may or may not be regarded as separate entities). (2004, 84)

To follow Hayles, collaborating with machines in this distributed cognition means that we – as she writes, 'in some sense' – become cyborgs. Writing in 2004, Hayles was not thinking of smartphones logging our every move. But even just as readers sharing the act of interpretation and cognition with a machine she wrote that we were constructed as cyborgs:

> Because electronic hypertexts are written and read in distributed cognitive environments, the reader necessarily is constructed as a cyborg, spliced into an integrated circuit with one or more intelligent machines. (Cyborg is of course a neologism coined from cybernetic organism, part organic being, part machine.) To be positioned as a cyborg is inevitably in some sense to become a cyborg, so electronic hypertexts, regardless of their content, tend toward cyborg subjectivity. (85)

Perhaps this is simply another way of saying we become quantified selves.

Gamified lives

Similar to the diaries Lejeune (2001) describes, self-tracking apps are always written in the present and always hold the promise of the next entry, the next logged item, the next steps. Even if you don't use Runkeeper for a year or two, it will keep your data and seamlessly connect it to your new runs if you start using the app again. There is a promise of eternity in this software, although we know that at some point the device will be broken or lost, and the software won't be kept updated forever. Wendy Hui Kyong Chun writes that software creates an 'enduring ephemeral': 'Through a process of constant regeneration, of constant "reading", it

DOI: 10.1057/9781137476661.0006

creates an enduring ephemeral that promises to last forever, even as it marches toward obscelescence/stasis' (2011, 137). When machines write our diaries, our human choices and life spans no longer decide when or whether a diary ends. On the contrary, we have online identities before we are born and well after we die (Leaver and Highfield 2014).

Studies suggest that most people do not track data over long periods, although there are certainly examples of people who do so. Participants in a study by John Rooksby and fellow researchers at the University of Glasgow tended to use trackers for short periods of time, often switching devices or tracking different aspects of their lives. Rooksby et.al. argue that 'personal tracking might best be understood as prospective rather than retrospective,' and that it is strongly tied to goals (2014, 1168).

Activity trackers and fitness apps often cite statistics about users who have successfully lost weight or become regular runners by using their app. So and so many percent of users who log in daily lose weight, My Fitness Pal tells us, coaxing us to come back, again and again, much as a game like World of Warcraft builds in mechanisms to keep us returning and paying our monthly fees (S. Rettberg 2008). The apps are designed to keep us interested, sending notifications to our phones if we have ignored them for too long. If I neglect to open Heyday's automatic photo journal, it pops up a notification on the home screen of my phone: 'You took 3 photos at 3 locations. Did you see anything interesting today?' If I gain weight the Withings scale app, Health Mate, uses a red font instead of a green one and gently chides me, 'Let's keep our eyes on the goal.' But these are framed as temporary setbacks towards an achievable goal. Lejeune (2001) wrote about the four ways in which diaries can end. Automatic journals and lifelogs cannot end. You can delete the app, and possibly delete your data, but there is no closure to the narratives these apps tell. There is no happily ever after, and even death will not conclude your Facebook timeline.

Many activity trackers use elements of gamification in the system mechanics. The basic premise of these trackers has a lot in common with games: you have a goal (lose three kilos or run a half-marathon) and you are given challenges through which you can earn points that move you towards that goal. The goal is outside of the game mechanics, but by using a wifi-connected scale or a location and motion tracking smart-phone app the physical and digital aspects of the game are connected. As in complex games, there can be several goals. Runkeeper lets you select or type in your own overall motivation, where one default is 'Live a long and healthy life', but you can also set specific goals such as 'Run 38 kms

DOI: 10.1057/9781137476661.0006

in a week', or 'Run 5k in under 30 minutes', which have progress bars, training plans explaining the steps that must be taken along the way and clearly defined points at which you have achieved your goal.

Paolo Pedercini argues that games are prime examples of the rationalisation Max Weber described in *The Protestant Ethic* and *The Spirit of Capitalism* at the end of the nineteenth century. 'If computer games', Pedercini (2014) writes, 'in their immense variety, have anything in common, that may be their compulsion for efficiency and control. Computer games are the aesthetic form of rationalization'. And yet despite the grind of immensely successful games such as Farmville where human relationships are rationalised to 'most helpful friend' rankings, there are many games that explore alternatives. Listing numerous alternative games, Pedercini (2014) calls for resistance: 'poetic wrenches have to be thrown in the works; gears and valves have to grow hair, start pulsing and breathing; algorithms must learn to tell stories and scream in pain'.

Ian Bogost writes about a 'rhetoric of failure' in games designed so that the player cannot win (2007, 85). One could put Tetris or Space Invaders in such a category – the blocks or missiles keep falling until the player fails to keep them at bay, meaning that you will always, ultimately, lose the game. The winning situation, if there is one, is to get a higher score than your friends. Perhaps, as Janet Murray wrote of Tetris, this is a metaphor for a typical American life (1997, 144). But the games Bogost discusses as having a rhetoric of failure are so-called serious games, games that clearly aim to make an argument through their gameplay. An example is Gonzala Frasca's *Kabul Kaboom*, a minigame where the player controls a figure from Picasso's anti-war painting *Guernica*: a mother, mouth upwards in a wail, holding an infant. The background is a low-resolution cameraphone picture of the sky over Kabul, lit up with bombs, similar to the many photos in the news around the time of the attacks on Afghanistan. Missiles and bread rain down from the sky and your goal is to try to catch bread rather than missiles, which of course is impossible. You will always die in this game. As I wrote in an analysis of this and other games about Bin Laden in 2003, 'Games such as these make a double move. First they claim that a current situation is a game. Then they say that this game cannot be won' (Walker 2003, 163). Lifelogging apps likewise claim that the current situation is a game, but these gamified lives of ours are games that will never end. There is no winning or losing situation, only a series of goals. Once one goal is achieved we must work towards the next.

DOI: 10.1057/9781137476661.0006

There are very few, if any, examples of lifelogging apps that resist the drive towards self improvement and rationalisation. There are individual art projects, but there is no *Kabul Kaboom* for lifelogging apps, not yet.

One app that does challenge the progress narrative is Carrot, 'the A.I. construct with a heart of weapons-grade plutonium' (meetcarrot.com). By mid-2014, Carrot has three apps: a to do app, an alarm clock and a fitness app. A to do list can be seen as a kind of diary, prospective rather than retrospective, but Carrot has more obvious game style mechanics than most to do apps, and gives you rewards and level ups when you complete tasks. However, Carrot has mood swings when you don't complete tasks, and although there's not really an ultimate goal to be achieved or a winning situation (there are always more tasks to add to your to do list) the rewards along the way are quite amusing. Early on, she gives you a kitten:

> GIFT_001. I bought you a kitten! No really. A real live kitten. He's sitting on server rack 13 right now, cleaning his paw. He's black and cute and so, so tiny.

Instead of an 'OK' button, the button you have to click to get back to your tasks says 'OH MY GOSH!' When you complete several tasks in a row, Carrot's textual response may be 'Astonishing. Simply astonishing.' Rewards continue to flow as you cross more and more tasks off your list: 'KITTEN_002. Your new kitten is awfully cute. What should we name him?' Your response screen shows two options: 'Bob Cat' and 'Captain Whiskers'. If you stop completing tasks, Carrot has mood swings. Bad mood swings. The screen background switches from white with blue accents to an angry black with red accents, and she grouches at you: 'It's been 6 hours since you last contributed to society.' Even if you complete tasks she'll be angry: 'You chose ... poorly.'

I used Carrot as my regular to do app for several weeks and enjoyed its sarcastic approach to time management and productivity. The mechanics of Carrot are basically the same as the mechanics of any other to do app, but by adding the sarcasm, the rewards and the mood swings, and of course the A.I. character's constant insults ('To-do list empty. Get something done, lazy human!'), it makes our obedience (or lack of obedience) to our apps even more visible.

DOI: 10.1057/9781137476661.0006

5

Quantified Selves

Abstract: *The title of this chapter is taken from the quantified self movement, where people track and analyse aspects of their lives such as steps, travels, productivity, location, glucose, heart rate, coffee intake, sleep and more to understand and improve themselves. Quantified self-representation has rapidly become common far beyond this movement, though: one in ten Americans owns an activity tracker such as a Fitbit or Nike Fuelband, and there are hundreds of other devices and apps to measure different aspects of our lives. This chapter considers what we can measure about ourselves and what we cannot measure, and the consequences of seeing ourselves as data bodies, using smart baby monitors, sex tracking and activity trackers as examples. Concepts discussed include dataism, the new aesthetic and machine vision.*

Rettberg, Jill Walker. *Seeing Ourselves Through Technology: How We Use Selfies, Blogs and Wearable Devices to See and Shape Ourselves.* Basingstoke: Palgrave Macmillan, 2014. DOI: 10.1057/9781137476661.0007.

Towards the end of 2013, I attended a meeting held by the Bergen Chamber of Commerce on social media marketing. Several hundred marketers ate lunch as they listened to a presenter explaining her company's successful Facebook marketing campaign. 'The wonderful thing about digital media,' she said, 'is that you can measure everything.' Her company was launching a new social media marketing strategy, and she was thrilled at how easily they were able to track their progress: how many likes each post received, the age groups who were following the page and how many times different kinds of posts were shared. Administrators of Facebook pages can see at a glance that more people click 'like' on certain kinds of post or on items posted at certain times of the day or of the week.

Being able to measure something gives us the sense that we can control it. We can work to improve it, whether it's a marketing campaign or our productivity or our health. Having measurements readily available can also make us forget about all the things we cannot measure.

There are currently different kinds of activity trackers commercially available, with names such as Fitbit, Nike Fuelband, Jawbone Up, Withings Pulse, Misfit Shine and many more. They are worn on wristbands, hung from necklaces or clipped onto pockets, and measure how many steps we take, how many stairs we climb, what our heart rates are or how we sleep. They sync to websites or phone apps in which graphs are generated and daily averages calculated. They connect to other apps, like My Fitness Pal in which you enter all the food you eat to compare your calorie intake with the calories your stepcounter tells you that you burn, or Runkeeper, which uses GPS to track your runs, or other devices such as Withings scale that uploads your weight to the Internet. There are blood pressure monitors for people concerned about their heart, glucose monitors for diabetics and heart rate monitors for amateur and professional athletes. There are to-do apps that show us how efficient we are and time monitors that track whether we're spending time using a word-processor or checking Facebook.

We don't typically think of these self-tracking tools as self-representations in the same way as we do self-portraits or diaries, but they do preserve and present images of us: images that are both very accurate and very narrow, whether they track steps, heart rate, productivity or location. Fifteen years ago, well before smartphones and Foursquare, I walked out on the balcony at a party and noticed a woman fiddling with a GPS, setting her coordinates. She told me that most people didn't

DOI: 10.1057/9781137476661.0007

understand why she liked to do that. But her grandmother did: 'Oh, I see, love,' her grandma had said, 'it's like a diary!' And that is exactly how this woman used her GPS – as another way of documenting her life and keeping memories.

I have a travel diary my grandmother kept during a trip by boat to Europe in the 1960s. There is nothing personal in the diary: each day there is simply a note of each port of call. Sometimes she would add what they ate for dinner. Today, Foursquare serves the same purpose for me. I check in at places I want to remember, or that I want to tell people about, and sometimes, often when I return to a city I have previously visited, I look back through my history, and the list jogs my memories so I remember much more than the simple names of cafés or sites that Foursquare reminds me of. This simple data, then, means more to me than to a random observer. When my grandmother looked at her sparse travel diary, she remembered her trip, whereas I only see a list of places and meals. Sometimes our own lists of data and the quantified charts that track aspects of our lives might even give us the sense of *punctum* that Barthes wrote of seeing in certain photographs, though others would see nothing but a *studium*.

A fantasy of knowing

'Self Knowledge Through Numbers' is the slogan of the Quantified Self movement, a group of people who use wearable devices, spreadsheets, notebooks and more to track and analyse data about themselves. The quantified self conferences, meetups and blogs showcase individuals' stories about how they have used self-tracking to improve their lives, become more productive, manage a disease, sleep better, lose weight, become fit and even find romance. Conferences, meetups and blogs host 'show and tell' talks where presenters explain what they did, how they did it and what they learnt. Many quantified selfers use consumer devices such as activity trackers or glucose monitors, but their analyses of the data provided tend to go beyond the standard visualisations provided by the brands' own websites or apps. Quantified selfers use spreadsheets, statistical tools and visualisation software to understand and present their data.

Although people have been tracking their personal data for centuries, the combination of data generated through wearable devices and online

DOI: 10.1057/9781137476661.0007

services that can automatically log personal data with our increasing ability to store and process large quantities of data has led to a surge of interest in personal tracking and data analysis. The interest isn't solely driven by technology. Society in general is increasingly invested in quantitative measures that we hope will allow us to improve our performance. My six-year-old daughter brought reports home from her Chicago Public School kindergarten class this spring telling us exactly what percentile she was in for reading and mathematics. I can go online and see a detailed 'report card' of her school, with precise numbers for ethnic and income diversity, truancy rates, children's average test scores and more. Back home in Norway there is less emphasis on standardised tests and quantitative comparisons of schools, but even here, standardised tests have been implemented for some grade levels. We can compare scores at the level of the child, the school, the district and even the country through the PISA scores. At the University of Bergen where I work, the Humanities Faculty works out whether to replace a professor who retires with a new professor in the same field or to use the resources elsewhere by annually feeding a complicated spreadsheet information such as how many credits students have taken in each discipline, how many articles and books were published by our colleagues in each field, how many PhD students have completed their degrees in which subjects and so on. If there is money to hire three new associate professors one year, the spreadsheet calculates which departments and fields need the jobs the most and presents the faculty board with a prioritised list. To be sure, this may be fairer than the old system, where, according to legend, whichever head of department wept the most convincingly in front of the dean got the new jobs, but it is also an interesting example of our increasing reliance on data and numbers above qualitative interpretation. This is the way we run our education systems, our companies and our lives now: by analysing the data. Of course we use data in our self-representations.

Our quantitative self-representations are not entirely objective, though the numbers, checkboxes and graphs give them that appearance. In reality, of course the data is fuzzy. When I use Nicolas Felton's app Reporter to record information about my days I might lie, a little, about the information I enter. It beeps and asks me to tell it whether I'm working or not when I'm actually on Facebook, but because I just spent an hour writing maybe I'll tell it I'm working anyway. Or I put my phone away at 11 pm, telling Reporter that I'm going to sleep, but get distracted and don't actually go to bed for another hour. Perhaps I really do write for eight hours

DOI: 10.1057/9781137476661.0007

one day but the five times the app prompts me to tell it what I'm doing I happen to be taking breaks, and I'm honest about my answers each time. Then Reporter will actually misrepresent me as not having worked that day. Sometimes we fudge the data to make ourselves look better (even just to ourselves) and other times we fudge it to represent ourselves in a way that feels more accurate, although it may not be exactly true.

When we slip an activity tracker onto our wrist rather than enter data manually, the output may feel less subjective. We have less direct control over it. The number of steps is precise – 9028 steps, not 'around nine thousand', although of course if we forget to put the tracker on and go for a bike ride, the step count may not reflect our true activity during a day. When I wore a Fitbit and later a Misfit Shine they produced graphs showing exactly how much deep and light sleep I got (though not what was really meant by those categories), how long it took me to fall asleep each night and on average, and how many times I woke during the night. I loved seeing all this information, although I had never before realised that these were things I wanted to know.

Quantitative self-representations can be like visualisations of big data, in that they, represent 'a fantasy of knowing, or total knowledge' (McCosker and Wilken 2014). We think that the numbers tell us the objective truth.

New parents are one group targeted by data tracking services. New parents are sleep-deprived, hormonally and emotionally all over the place, and desperate to get some sleep and keep their babies safe. In 2008 I used the TrixieTracker website to track my four-month-old baby's sleep patterns (J.W. Rettberg 2009). Being sleep-deprived, I had read what felt like dozens of books about helping babies sleep regularly and most of them recommended keeping track of your baby's natural schedule to look for patterns. Then, in theory, you could figure out how to get your baby on a schedule that let you get more sleep. Does the baby sleep better if her bedtime is earlier or later? Does she wake more or less frequently during the night if you keep her awake and active for several hours before bedtime? Does she fall asleep more quickly if she just ate or if she played before being put down? I desperately wanted answers that would let me (and my baby) get more sleep.

TrixieTracker wasn't automatic. I had to click a button on the website (which I could access from my smartphone) to register when I put our baby down in her crib, when she actually fell asleep and when she woke up. I could enter information about when she ate and from which breast

DOI: 10.1057/9781137476661.0007

she nursed and about the contents of her nappies. Some parents tracked this sort of information about their babies long before there were digital aids. Having lunch in a café with a group of other mothers and babies, I noticed one of the other mothers pull out a sheet of graph paper with a carefully colour-coded chart. When I asked her about it, she showed me how she used different colours for sleep and awake time, and also marked nappy changes and feedings. She had kept these charts faithfully for each of her babies, and said she found them very helpful. As she spoke, she marked the chart to show that she had fed her baby 10 minutes earlier.

I used TrixieTracker for a few months and enjoyed seeing the charts it generated. Ultimately I didn't find any useful patterns, other than the rather obvious finding that as our baby grew older she fell asleep more easily and woke less frequently during the night. I probably would have noticed that without the charts, but I enjoyed having the visual material to look at. I even put a printout of one of the charts in my baby's baby journal.

Tracking quantitative information about babies is taken for granted today, but systematic weighing of newborns at birth did not begin until the late eighteenth and early nineteenth century (Oppenheimer 2013, 114), and weighing babies and children at regular intervals was not introduced until the mid-nineteenth century (115). For today's parents, measuring babies starts during pregnancy, when each doctor's visit includes weighing in, measuring the height of the uterus and a blood test. Results are entered into a journal, marked on a chart showing normal growth curves and very clearly measured as normal or concerning. Once the baby is born, this quantitative measurement transfers from the mother to the baby. The baby's weight and length at birth are proudly announced to friends and family. They are measured again at each visit to the doctor or nurse, and the medical professional plots the data onto a standardised growth curve, pronouncing at which percentile of the population the baby weighs in at. If the baby doesn't gain weight at the expected rate, parents are asked to feed the baby more, to nurse more frequently or in a different way or to supplement with formula. If the low growth rate persists the doctor will look for other causes. Measuring babies and children is seen as an important part of preventative health care today.

A friend told me about her deep guilt when she realised that her two-week-old baby had not gained back her birth weight. 'I was starving my baby,' she sobbed. New parents experience real anxiety – and conversely real comfort – from seeing objectively whether their baby is thriving or

DOI: 10.1057/9781137476661.0007

not. When you have a fussy or colicky baby that cries inconsolably for hours every day, it is comforting to be told by a medical professional that your baby is thriving, which generally means that the measurements show that the baby is gaining weight just as expected. But the desire for clear, objective, rational information about your baby can get out of hand. When my oldest child was a few weeks old, another new mother mentioned that her baby hadn't gained much weight in the last week. 'How do you know?' I asked. She explained that she came in to the clinic twice a week just to weigh her baby. It hadn't even occurred to me that this was a possibility or something you might want to do, and the nurse had told me that my baby's growth was just fine, but hearing about the other mother's diligence I immediately felt guilty for not having worried about my baby's weight. So I started coming in twice a week and got more and more worried as I saw my baby had no weight gain at all for several days. Fortunately, the nurse caught me at it and explained that weight fluctuates from day to day and that there is really no point in weighing a healthy baby too often. It does no good, and often does harm in that it worries the parents unnecessarily. I stopped coming in between appointments and my baby was fine.

Today's new mothers can buy baby scales that connect to the Internet and generate growth curves you can view on your smartphone. The Withings Baby Scale even connects to Nestlé's capsule-based baby formula making machine, the BabyNes, so you can use one app to monitor your baby's growth *and* to know how many bottles of milk you prepare for the baby. You can annotate the data to show how much your baby actually drank, too. Following EU law, Nestlé of course notes in their marketing of the system that breastfeeding is the ideal nourishment for your baby, but the very existence of this app showcases how the perceived *objectivity* of technology and quantitative measurements can be seductive. The ease of measuring how much formula a baby drinks is one of the reasons why bottle feeding for a long time was preferred to breastfeeding by the medical establishment. You can weigh a baby before and after it is breastfed to measure how much milk it drank, but this is more cumbersome than simply looking at the millilitre markings on a bottle of milk.

Baby monitors have also become quantified. Wearable devices for babies include the Mimo Baby Monitor where babies wear a specially designed onesie (the 'Kimono') which has a soft rubber spot that holds a monitor, called the 'Turtle'. This connects to a web service that sends data about the baby's breathing, body temperature and movements to an

DOI: 10.1057/9781137476661.0007

app for a smartphone. Graphs showing the waves of regular breathing are generated, and alerts sound to let you know if the baby is restless, too cold or too hot or sleeping on his tummy instead of his back or side. Trends and analytics can be viewed over time. The Sproutling ankle band, due to go to market in late 2014, will alert you when your baby is about to wake up. Mats that monitor babies' breath and similar technologies are already in use in hospitals and at home for premature babies or babies who are particularly at risk for SIDS or other medical problems, but they are now being marketed to parents of healthy babies as though every baby needs this kind of constant medical monitoring.

Dataism and subjective data visualisation

Dataism is José van Dijck's term for the common assumption that people and behaviours can be adequately represented by quantitative means and 'big data.' She writes that 'the ideology of *dataism* shows characteristics of a widespread *belief* in the objective quantification and potential tracking of all kinds of human behavior and sociality through online media technologies' (van Dijck 2014). Often big data analysis works, in the sense that it can be used to predict buying patterns or personality traits, and van Dijck cites a number of scholarly articles showing direct connections between data such as tweets and personality traits or between liked pages on Facebook and sexual preferences. Dataism is becoming 'a belief in a new gold standard of knowledge about human behavior', van Dijck writes, and argues that it is crucial to be aware of the different reasons for and contexts within which data is gathered. We also need to realise that data is interpreted by analysts.

The data gathered about us by our devices becomes an artifact that is separate from us and can be viewed at a distance. At the same time, it represents us, or a part of our lives. Minna Ruckenstein (2014) calls this personal data a *data double*, a term taken from a much-cited article in surveillance studies where Kevin D. Haggerty and Richard V. Ericson use Deleuze and Guattari to analyse the ways in which once separate flows of information about individuals are put together:

> This assemblage operates by abstracting human bodies from their territorial settings and separating them into a series of discrete flows. These flows are then reassembled into distinct 'data doubles' which can be scrutinized and targeted for intervention. (Haggerty and Ericson 2000, 606)

DOI: 10.1057/9781137476661.0007

Heart-rate variability monitors can indicate levels of stress and recovery, and Ruckenstein's survey looked at how a group of users of such monitors reacted to the personal data collected about their heart-rate variations using a monitor. Although the users did negotiate and interpret their data doubles, comparing the data to experiences in their lives during the period they had worn the monitors, Ruckenstein (2014) notes that

> Significantly, data visualizations were interpreted by research participants as more 'factual' or 'credible' insights into their daily lives than their subjective experiences. This intertwines with the deeply-rooted cultural notion that 'seeing' makes knowledge reliable and trustworthy.

The way in which we choose to visualise data is important. Data, Johanna Drucker (2011) writes, is assumed to be a ' "given" able to be recorded and observed'. She proposes that instead of talking about data, we should use the term *capta*, which would emphasise a constructivist approach: capta is *taken* from reality, while data is conceived as *given*, objective. Similarly, Annette Markham (2013b) notes how the meaning of the term data 'gradually shifted from a description of that which precedes argument to that which is pre–analytical and pre–semantic. Put differently, data is beyond argument. It always exists, no matter how it might be interpreted. Data has an incontrovertible "itness"'. Susan Sontag notes something similar of our assumptions about the reality of photographs:

> What is written about a person or an event is frankly an interpretation, as are handmade visual statements, like paintings and drawings. Photographed images do not seem to be statements about the world so much as pieces of it, miniatures of reality that anyone can make or acquire. (1973, 4)

Of course, as Markham and Sontag also argue, neither data nor photographs are truly 'pieces of the world' devoid of interpretation. They are representations, but ones that we tend to find more authoritative than more obviously qualitative representations.

An alternative approach is taken by many francophone theorists, who use the term digital traces (*traces numeriques*) to refer to the tracks we leave behind us when we use digital media. Tyler Butler Reigeluth (2014, 249) explains that a trace 'corresponds to some minute detail or seemingly insignificant fragment such as the chemist's residue, the detective's clue, the historian's indices, or the psychoanalyst's symbol,' and although the meaning of the word *trace* in French doesn't completely correspond to the same word in English, it does seem that the concept of digital

DOI: 10.1057/9781137476661.0007

traces carries with it more uncertainty and subjectivity than our English *data*. We do not take the traces of a person (footsteps in the snow, steps measured by a Fitbit) as being the same as the person herself. Or as Drucker (2011) puts it,

> Rendering *observation* (the act of creating a statistical, empirical, or subjective account or image) as if it were *the same as the phenomena observed* collapses the critical distance between the phenomenal world and its interpretation, undoing the basis of interpretation on which humanistic knowledge production is based.

Drucker argues that to visualise subjective data (or capta, in her terminology), we need subjective, qualitative graphics as well. Perhaps we could think of the Fitbit's glowing flower that grows throughout the day the more that you move as a somewhat subjective visualisation of your activity. The Misfit Shine shows little glowing dots instead of precise step counts. The Withing Activité has an analogue clock face with a pointer moving clockwise from 0 to 100 to show whether the user has taken enough steps that day. These less precise visualisations show a desire to humanise our data, although the premise is still that you are at a measurable point on your way to a fixed goal.

Measure more

I put my hand up at the Chamber of Commerce meeting, to ask the social media marketers what they would do if they found that the measurements they had access to weren't telling them everything they needed to know. 'Measure your results, adjust your actions, and measure again,' said the presenter.

Another of the presenters spoke up. It was Anders Brenna, a Norwegian technology expert who is highly influential in Norwegian social media circles. 'You just need more measurement points,' he said. 'If you look at a map of weather stations,' he continued, 'you will see that they are close together in some parts of the world and very far apart in other parts of the world. When they put more weather stations in, the weather forecasts become more accurate.'

Of course this is true, up to a point. More measurements and more different kinds of measurement can make forecasts and analyses more accurate, or more appealing. Often, extra measurements are crowd-

DOI: 10.1057/9781137476661.0007

sourced. Minutely, a weather forecasting app, combines traditional forecasts with allowing users to report the weather in their own location by selecting an icon with a brief description: Sunny, Mostly Sunny, Overcast, Drizzle and so on. There's also an option to share a photo and type in a brief message. This potentially combines a subjective sense of the weather with the automated reports, but in practice the shared weather is hidden in the interface, and seeing other peoples' reports is not easy. Still, being able to correct the weather app and tell it (and potentially other users) that in fact it is not raining where I am can feel satisfying. The ability to share one's personal weather report and comments directly to Twitter or Facebook also suggest that this feature is more about self-expression than about the subjective human experiential data actually influencing the machine.

Tracking data isn't simply about the data, either. Once we have personal, quantified data about ourselves, we look at it and we interpret it. We use the data to adjust the stories we already tell ourselves about our lives, and we use our stories about our lives to adjust, excuse or understand our data. Ruckenstein writes that 'once visualized, the data generates new kinds of affective ties between people and their measured actions and reactions.' She continues, referencing a study by Bjarke Oxlund (2012, 50): 'For instance, pedometer users can cherish the steps they have taken and develop a more affective relationship either to their walking or the steps taken; numbers acquire qualities that promote new kinds of walking-related practices' (Ruckenstein 2014). In her own study where participants tracked their heart-rate variability, Ruckenstein found the same 'affective ties,' and notes that having the data can make people feel more pride in what they do:

> Similarly, the monitoring of the quality of sleep through heart-rate variability measurements can deepen affective relations to one's body. When sleeping is subjected to tracking, it becomes an activity, or even a competence, that people feel that they are good at. On the other hand, the tired body, pinned down by personal analytics, reflects exhaustion caused by the energy that people put into work and care for others, thereby making their contributions visible and of value. (Ruckenstein 2014)

Another study of users of activity trackers found something similar, when informants used their data almost as vindication: 'they were aggrieved by the amount of activity they were doing and somehow wanted to underline their effort' (Rooksby et al. 2014, 1168).

DOI: 10.1057/9781137476661.0007

Self-tracking can be used as a means of power, whether to make contributions visible or to fight back against surveillance. UPS drivers are monitored in great detail throughout their workday: digital equipment in their trucks track when parcels are delivered, how long the truck is stopped, whether the seat belt is fastened, how much the truck backs up and more. On 1 July 2010, the drivers' union, Teamsters for a Democratic Union (TDU), published a printable 'Package car driver OJS tracking sheet' on their website to allow drivers to track themselves and their supervisors so as to have documentation if their employers attempted to hold them to a measured speed of delivery that is not representative of a normal work day. 'Track the Supervisor like They Track You,' a union representative says on the website. This is what Steve Mann has dubbed 'sousveillance': ordinary citizens watching authorities rather than the other way around (Mann, Nolan, and Wellman 2003).

What we cannot measure

The sex tracking app SpreadSheets offers a striking example of how little our devices can really measure. Spreadsheets is an iPhone app that promises to measure and quantify our sexual activity. Similar to one of its forerunners, Bedposted.com, its purpose is to create a log of each time you have sex, but while Bedposted.com required you to enter the information yourself (J.W. Rettberg 2014, 87–8), Spreadsheets monitors your sex life automatically. That is, Spreadsheets tracks every aspect of sex that an iPhone can automatically track when placed on a bed: frequency of thrusts, total duration of thrusting activity and the decibel levels of the participants in the act. That's really all an iPhone can automatically measure about sex: motion, sound and when that motion and sound begins and ends. As Whitney Erin Boesel (2013) points out in a blog post to *Cyborgology*, that means that this app can only measure a very heteronormative idea of sex as thrusting penetration.

The Spreadsheets app applies a technological filter to its representation of sex. The representation is constrained by what an iPhone can measure. Interestingly enough, though, the way a machine – or specifically a smartphone in the early twenty-first century – can understand or perceive sex is very close to a strong cultural understanding of sex that we are familiar with from traditional pornography. Sex seen through this cultural filter is all about thrusting hard and fast, screaming loudly and keeping at it for as long as possible. But we all know that that is not all there is to sex – far from it. Notably Spreadsheets cannot perceive aspects of sex that do not involve thrusting or loud vocalisation, such as caresses, kisses or whispers. And importantly, Spreadsheets can do nothing to measure our emotions during lovemaking.

Following Anders Brenna's example of the weather stations, we might argue that all Spreadsheets needs to do is to install more measuring stations and measure more. It is certainly possible to imagine specialised appendages that could be plugged into a smartphone and worn on or inserted into bodies to measure other aspects of sex than thrusts and decibels. They could use the 'happiness blankets' that British Airways used to market their flights in June 2014: in a video advertisement, passengers wore headbands that measured their brainwaves, and the blankets, which had threads of LEDs woven through them, glowed red when passengers were anxious and blue when they were calm and happy (British Airways 2014). A device could even analyse users' blood to gauge something of their emotional arousal. No doubt such devices are already used in medical research. Last year, a Dutch team of researchers developed a tool to automatically log unconscious emotions by analysing physiological data, arguing that 'To offer capabilities that are superior to diaries, lifelogging applications should try to capture the complete experiences of people including data from both their external and internal worlds' (Ivonin et al., 2012). But could even a fastidiously detailed computational analysis of a sexual encounter represent it in a way that felt meaningful to the people involved?

If we see ourselves and expect to be seen as data bodies, as quantifiable selves, what do we see? What is left out? Would we want a 'happiness blanket' to tell everyone around us whether we are calm or anxious? Do we want automated diaries to tell us about emotions we aren't even aware of?

The pleasure of control

Works of fiction can critique society and technology as strongly as scholarship or critical works, and often more evocatively and memorably. Dave Eggers novel *The Circle* (2013) tells the story of Mae, who begins to work for The Circle, a company that is a sort of amalgamate of our Facebook and Google, but even more sinister. Mae is rapidly fitted with various tracking devices, from a wristband that monitors her health

DOI: 10.1057/9781137476661.0007

to productivity trackers to monitor her efficiency in responding to customer calls. In her first weeks she is surprised at some of the monitoring, but after a disciplinary conversation with her superiors, Josiah and Denise, who question her lack of involvement in social media, she throws herself into it wholeheartedly and eventually goes 'transparent', wearing a video camera that streams to the Internet at all times. 'Privacy is theft', she declares, and 'Sharing is caring'. The main characters use wearable devices constantly, and their different comfort levels with this are interesting to follow. Mae enjoys the objectivity of the devices that track her.

> She knew her heart rate and knew it was right. She knew her step count, almost 8,200 that day, and knew that she could get to 10,000 with ease. She knew she was properly hydrated and that her caloric intake that day was within accepted norms for someone of her body-mass index. It occurred to her, in a moment of sudden clarity, that what had always caused her anxiety, or stress, or worry, was not any one force, nothing independent and external – it wasn't danger to herself or the constant calamity of other people and their problems. It was internal: it was subjective, it was *not knowing*. It wasn't that she had an argument with a friend or was called on the carpet by Josiah and Denise: it was not knowing what it meant, not knowing their plans, not knowing the consequences, the future. If she knew these, she would be calm. (194)

Mae loves *knowing*, and believes that *not knowing* is what has caused her stress in the past. This idea that technology can be a neutral, objective observer that can alleviate the uncertainty of human perception is alluring to many. As Melissa Gregg (2014) writes about productivity apps, they 'facilitate the pleasure of time management, which is ultimately the pleasure of control'. Gregg continues by noting that productivity apps 'offer strategies for closure and containment, from shutting down email and non-essential communication to identifying peak performance periods and ideal moments for efficiency.'

Closure and containment, knowing rather than not knowing, are seductive possibilities to many. Most activity trackers do not offer a great deal more than telling us how many steps we walk each day, but they also convert this into an estimation of calories burned and invite us to enter information about the calories we eat. This is a messy business at best. Most of the calorie tracking sites have databases of foods, and US fast food or grocery store brands are far better documented than foods from other countries or homemade food. If you search MyFitnessPal for

DOI: 10.1057/9781137476661.0007

'tomato soup' you get a list of various 'tomato soups' in the database, some entered by users and some harvested from companies' information about the foods they sell. There's some user's homemade soup at 156 calories a cup and Campbell's canned tomato soup at 110 calories for half a cup. Panera's creamy tomato soup is 210 calories for 12 oz and Cosi's is 401 calories for 10 ounces. A user may not be sure which soup she is eating or exactly how many ounces or cups she has, and user-entered nutrition information for soup or any other dish may be completely wrong, but despite any doubt in the process of entering this data, once it is entered it is treated as exactly accurate. Calories are added up precisely, steps are counted, and you are told precisely how many calories too many or too few you have eaten. When you click 'finished logging for today' the app quickly calculates what you would weigh in five weeks if each day was like today. Any uncertainty is erased by the apparent precision of the data.

The Withings app on my phone, HealthMate, pulls in data from MyFitnessPal and our Withings 'smart scale' and uses this to generate even more graphs. It tells me that at 10 am my calorie intake is 228 calories and my calorie outtake is 789. I should probably have something to eat. The air quality around my bathroom scale is good, at least as measured by CO_2, which appears to be the only aspect of air quality the scale measures, and the temperature in my bathroom is 19.6 °C. It tells me my heart rate the last time I weighed myself and my body fat percentage. My Fitbit told me how often I had woken during the night, and my Misfit Shine told me whether my sleep had been 'light' or 'heavy'.

Most of this data is useless, mere decoration, eye candy. Why keep detailed daily logs of my heart rate when I step on the scales or the temperature in the bathroom? Why know how much 'deep sleep' I got when nothing on the Misfit website can explain what that term means, or what might be optimal? If I am a data body, which data is meaningful?

Machine vision

When we use devices to represent ourselves, we rely on what the devices are able to measure. The step monitor doesn't really measure how many steps I take, it measures how often it moves in a way that tends to correlate to the way the device would move if a human, wearing it, took a step. My waving it up and down in a certain pattern can trick it into thinking

DOI: 10.1057/9781137476661.0007

I took more steps and my forgetting to carry it with me means it doesn't know about all the steps I take. And yet it continues to appear absolutely confident about my calorie outtake for the day.

In April 2011 iPhones running iOs 4 were found to be tracking all location data (up to 100 cell tower ID points a day) and saving this, unencrypted, to any computer the user synced the phone with (Arthur 2011). James Bridle is a British artist and designer who decided to exploit his own data, so he downloaded all the location information that his phone had been collecting without his knowledge and created a book full of maps of his whereabouts over the last year. The book is titled *Where the F**k Was I?* because Bridle found that he did not, in fact, remember all the places that the phone had registered him as visiting. The book of maps was not a representation of his experience, Bridle (2011) wrote, it was the experience of the phone itself:

> This digital memory sits somewhere between experience and non-experience; it is also an approximation; it is also a lie. These location records do not show where I was, but an approximation based on the device's own idea of place, its own way of seeing. They cross-reference me with digital infrastructure, with cell towers and wireless networks, with points created by others in its database. Where I correlate location with physical landmarks, friends and personal experiences, the algorithms latch onto invisible, virtual spaces, and the extant memories of strangers.

In this case, the human user did not know that the data was being collected and saved and did not consciously contribute to it. Other location-based services, like Foursquare, or its forerunner, Gowalla (Hooper and Rettberg 2011) require users to check in manually, deliberately choosing to make a note of having been in a specific location. Rather than location-tracking, this is known as location-sharing (Cramer, Rost, and Holmquist 2011, 57). Users don't check into every place they are. If you search, you can easily find etiquette guides posted on blogs, ironically or earnestly warning you not to check in to places that are boring (the gas station or grocery store), creepy (a brothel) or insensitive (a funeral home). Others warn that you risk being targeted by muggers if you check in at a bank or by stalkers if you check in at your home. A list of places you've checked into becomes a kind of curated self-representation, and as Lindqvist et.al. note, users choose not to check into places they feel embarrassed about or would rather not publically share: a fast food restaurant or a strip club, for instance, although not all users find these locales embarrassing (Lindqvist et al. 2011). The reasons for choosing to check in are varied. Some checkins are purely pragmatic, to coordinate with friends, but there are many other reasons for checking in, such as self-representation, boredom, playing a game, wanting to bookmark a place for future reference (Cramer, Rost, and Holmquist 2011), or 'documenting habits and sharing new experiences' (Hooper and Rettberg 2011). Venues on Foursquare are user-created and do not always have a one-to-one relationship with 'real' places. Sometimes checkins are deliberate rhetorical or communicative acts rather than statements of presence. For instance, during the heat wave in New York in the Summer of 2010, the 'Heatpocalypse NYC' received 9426 check-ins (Cramer, Rost, and Holmquist 2011, 62). In the Netherlands, game scholar René Glas describes how an abandoned high school inhabited by squatters was given the Foursquare name 'Hangout for idlers, potential criminals and people who've lost their ways' (2011, 12). When you use Foursquare you are invited to add 'tips' about venues for other users, and the prompt when you click on the 'Add a tip' button gives advice on how to write a tip: 'For example: Get the table by the front window for some of the best people watching in the city.' Tips users have left for the abandoned high school instead discuss how the local government has allowed the neighbourhood to become impoverished (Glas 2011, 13).

Individuals can create lists on Foursquare, and this can also be used as a form of self-expression. A literary example is *Derby [2061]*, a science fiction story created by the UK design agency Mudlark that is told through Foursquare. 50 fictional future Foursquare venues were created in the same geographical locale as present-day places in the town of Derby, and the story's protagonist, 'Girl X', has left tips in each place that taken together give an impression of a future society, set in the year 2061. Following our Foursquare friends we can similarly glean a partial story of their lives, though usually the story is far less cohesive than that told in *Derby [2061]*.

In 2014, Foursquare moved to 'passive location-sharing' with the new app Swarm. Rather than needing to check in, Swarm shares your approximate location with friends. A few months later, the Foursquare app also changed, rebranding itself as a recommendation engine primarily for restaurants rather than as a social travelogue. Although Swarm does still allow users to check in manually and to create new places, the changes signal a shift from human-generated to machine-generated self-representations, which we also see in other areas. Foursquare and Swarm

DOI: 10.1057/9781137476661.0007

are moving away from being shared diaries to being commercial market-ing platforms that represent us to our friends to convince our friends to buy certain services rather than others.

A few months after James Bridle created the book from his iPhone location log he wrote a blog post proposing the term 'the new aesthetic' to describe artistic and aesthetic projects that play with the idea of aesthetics that is created for or by machines (Bridle 2014). Rather than using words, Bridle states his case by gathering together groups of images of artworks and design.

One of Bridle's examples is CV Dazzle makeup, which is intended to be used in protests and riots where the human users do not want their faces to be recognised as human faces by surveillance cameras and face recog-nition software. Similarly, military aircraft and drones may have huge pixels painted on top to camouflage them from surveillance systems in satellites. If we are adjusting the way we express ourselves so that it can be read by machines, are we really speaking primarily to the machines and not to each other? Even if we are creating something for ourselves or for other humans, we have to mould our expression to what the devices we are using can perceive. Who—or what—are our self representations addressing?

DOI: 10.1057/9781137476661.0007

6
Privacy and Surveillance

Abstract: *In addition to our intended self-representations, our digital traces are being gathered by entities far beyond our control: government agencies, commercial companies, data brokers and possibly criminals. We have little or no access to these representations of us, although the data that shapes them comes from us. Foucault's idea of the panopticon is frequently mentioned in discussions of surveillance, but the practices of surveillance are changing yet again. Employers and insurers are just starting to ask us to willingly agree to constant surveillance of certain aspects of our life: our driving or our health, and in return we are promised discounts if we prove ourselves worthy. How can we create a balance between using our machines to see ourselves and being forced to be seen by machines?*

Rettberg, Jill Walker. *Seeing Ourselves Through Technology: How We Use Selfies, Blogs and Wearable Devices to See and Shape Ourselves.* Basingstoke: Palgrave Macmillan, 2014. DOI: 10.1057/9781137476661.0008.

Most of this book has been about how we as individuals create self-representations of ourselves for our own use and to share with each other, but each of us is also represented by other entities in ways that we cannot fully access. Governments collect data about us, as do many different commercial companies. Data brokers combine information about each of us and sell profiles of us to other companies. Commercial websites like Facebook or Amazon generate representations of me based on my data. We live in a time that is teaching each of us that constantly being monitored is normal and even to our benefit.

In this final chapter I write about the times that photos of us are coerced and used as disciplinary tools. I write about data brokers and how commercial companies are gathering our data and creating their own self-representations of us that we are not allowed to see. Finally, I write about the ways surveillance and tracking are used as tools for power, showing how Foucault's concept of the panopticon is changing as we today often knowingly allow ourselves to be watched.

Forced portraits

One of the most frequent reasons given for enjoying taking selfies is that it allows the subject full control over the photographic process, from deciding to take a photo, to choosing the angle and expression, to editing the image to choosing which photos to share with others. As Susan Sontag (1973) noted, 'photography is power' (8). Sontag writes, 'To photograph is to appropriate the thing photographed. It means putting oneself into a certain relation to the world that feels like knowledge – and, therefore, like power' (3). A few pages later she states, 'There is an aggression implicit in every use of the camera' (6).

Photos are regularly used against the subject's will as a form of discipline: police mugshots, the compulsory photographs non-US citizens undergo when entering the United States, driver's license photographs and photographs taken by the police during riots. Personal photographs can also be co-opted by authorities, for example, in an immigration process when an immigrant may have to prove that a marriage or relationship is authentic by providing personal photographs of the couple together over a period of time. Failing to have the expected photographs means that you are seen as suspicious. Photographs are not only used as weapons or disciplinary tools by authorities, but can also become weap-

DOI: 10.1057/9781137476661.0008

ons that can be turned against authorities or against a peer. A bystander's video of police brutality or a soldier's photo of a man being tortured can lead to widespread condemnation of police actions or of military interrogation practices. A nude photograph taken consensually during a love affair may be used for revenge after a breakup or for blackmail if it falls into the wrong hands.

Governments have kept census records about populations for many centuries. Today's records are far more extensive.

Who the advertisers think I am

Your data is extremely valuable to companies that want to sell you things or to organisations that want to convince you to support their agenda. You can easily see some of the consequences of your data being tracked. For example, when I spent a lot of time reading about activity trackers as research for this book, I started seeing ads for activity trackers on many different sites, including Facebook. In addition to data gathered from your web surfing habits, sites such as Facebook and Google use the demographic information you explicitly give them and information they glean from your status updates, private messages and email to customise your news feed and the ads they show you. If you switch your status to 'Engaged,' you will immediately be shown ads for wedding dresses and caterers. If you are a woman over 40, you will see ads for wrinkle cream and botox. The recently married will see ads about pregnancy and baby products, whereas those who have been married for a year without posting anything about being pregnant will likely see ads for fertility aids.

Just tracking what you buy can tell marketers a lot about you, as we saw in the case reported in 2012 where Target sent a teenager ads for maternity clothes based on what she'd been buying (apparently pregnant women buy more vitamins and lotions in the first two trimesters than an average woman does), in practice announcing the girl's pregnancy to her family before she had told them about it (Hill 2012). Sociologist Janet Vertesi (2014) wrote about how she tried to keep her recent pregnancy completely hidden from data brokers. It was a lot more complicated than you might think. She not only had to never mention the pregnancy on social media, even in private messages (which are also tracked for marketing data), but also couldn't browse baby-related sites online or buy anything baby-related using a credit card. Avoiding being tracked and profiled by data brokers is

DOI: 10.1057/9781137476661.0008

not easy to do. In *Dragnet Nation*, Julia Angwin (2014) writes about how she tries to keep her data private, and she concludes that to not be tracked you have to have very sophisticated technical knowledge or have a lot of money. As Vertesi points out, many of the strategies you might legitimately use to stay private – such as using encryption or using cash instead of credit cards – are also likely to flag you as a potential criminal.

The Timeline that Facebook introduced in 2011 is an interesting narrativisation of our lives, but it is also a goldmine for harvesting our 'life events', from weddings and births to moving house or getting a new job – or even breaking a leg or having braces removed from our teeth. 'Life events' are valued by data brokers who gather data about us from multiple sources and sell it to marketers. If you can locate the exact people who will be most likely to buy your product, whether that is pregnant women or people who have just bought a new house, and you market directly to them, you are likely to sell more products.

You don't even have to be online to have your data tracked. Companies track your purchases using loyalty cards or simply taking note of the credit card you use to make a purchase. There are companies that drive around taking photos of every car they come across and its license plate, creating a gigantic database of the location of millions of cars. The data is primarily intended for repossession of cars whose owners have not paid their car loans, but can also be used for many other purposes (Angwin 2014, 27). If you have a digital thermostat or smoke detector made by Nest, a company purchased by Google in 2014, Google has access to continuous information about the temperature or CO_2 levels in your home, which can for instance be used to track when people are present.

In Europe, privacy legislation limits the ways companies can use and connect personal data, and individuals have the right to see the data collected about them, but in the United States and many other countries commercial data collection is largely unregulated. The boundaries between government and commercial data collection are not always watertight. We know that the NSA gets data about us from commercial sites, and commercial data brokers add public data such as drivers license records or moving records to their data profiles of us. Some data we might think should be non-commercial, like data about children in public schools, is actually collected by private companies that run learning management systems, administer tests or provide educational software. Using this data can help children learn more easily. For instance, software will easily be able to track whether an individual child tends to

DOI: 10.1057/9781137476661.0008

persevere at a challenging task or whether he or she will give up quickly, and so the learning activities can be adjusted to that child's learning style. But the use of this data is unregulated in many parts of the world and could be sold to marketers and data brokers.

When today's six-year-olds finish high school, an astoundingly detailed representation of their lives at school will exist, and we don't yet know who will be able to access it. Depending on which country children live in, they may or may not have the right to see their own records. Information about their test scores, disciplinary issues, absences, tardiness, learning styles, health, home situation and personality from the time they were in preschool until they graduate may or may not be shared with marketers, insurance companies, potential employers, courts of law, the police and college admissions boards.

Dave Eggers imagines this data analysed in real time to produce continuously updated rankings of all students in the United States. Why stop at saying that a six year old is in such and such a percentile for reading? If Ivy League colleges admit 12,000 students a year, wouldn't parents love to know whether or not their child was in the top 12,000 students for their age? 'Once we get full participation from all schools and districts,' the representative from the ubiquitous social network service The Circle enthusiastically explains in Eggers's novel, 'we'll be able to keep daily rankings, with every test, every pop quiz incorporated instantly' (Eggers 2013, 341).

With current EU legislation, the individual has the right to see his or her own records, but not necessarily in a useful format. When I requested my information from my Norwegian cell phone provider they sent me 30 pages of printed times, dates, locations and phone numbers I had called over the previous three months. I assume it was printed rather than digital because it is far less useful to me on paper than in a format I could graph or analyse on a computer. Similarly, when I requested my hospital journals they were sent on paper, and I had to pay a fee for the photocopying. In the United States and many other countries individuals do not have the right to see data collected about them, although some companies will comply to some extent (Angwin 2014, 86–9).

Power and discipline

Foucault's theories of discipline are often referenced both in discussions of surveillance and of selfies and self-representations. In discussions of

DOI: 10.1057/9781137476661.0008

self-representation, theorists are interested in Foucault's ideas about 'technologies of the self,' which Foucault (1988) writes 'permit individuals to effect by their own means or with the help of others a certain number of operations on their own bodies and souls, thoughts, conduct, and way of being, so as to transform themselves in order to attain a certain state of happiness, purity, wisdom, perfection, or immortality' (18). In a study of NSFW (not safe for work) blogs where women and men shared erotic photos they had taken of themselves, Kathrin Tiidenberg (2014) invokes Foucault's self-cultivation, noting how an informant expressed that 'self-shooting gave her a way to care for herself and increase her self-awareness.' Through photographing herself, this woman developed a 'new gaze' that 'taught her to feel sexy in her body, but it also altered her material body-practices in terms of how she held herself, how she dressed and accessorized, whether she used make-up and how long she let her hair grow.' Or as Jodi Dean (2010) glosses Foucault's notion, 'Foucault's technologies of the self rely on the installation of a gaze, of the perspective of another before whom the subject imagines itself' (54).

Surveillance scholars on the other hand rarely fail to mention Foucault's theories of another aspect of power, a more direct gaze, or as Foucault (1988) writes: 'technologies of power, which determine the conduct of individuals and submit them to certain ends or domination, an objectivizing of the subject' (18).

Foucault wrote about Bentham's design for a wheel-shaped prison building where the gaolers would sit in the middle and be able to see each prisoner in his individual cell around the perimeter of the circle. The prisoners would not be able to see each other and would always know that they *might* be being watched. That knowledge would keep them disciplined, always behaving as the gaolers required.

> All that is needed, then, is to place a supervisor in a central tower and to shut up in each cell a madman, a patient, a condemned man, a worker or a schoolboy. By the effect of backlighting, one can observe from the tower, standing out precisely against the light, the small captive shadows in the cells of the periphery. They are like so many cages, so many small theatres, in which each actor is alone, perfectly individualized and constantly visible. The panoptic mechanism arranges spatial unities that make it possible to see constantly and to recognize immediately. In short, it reverses the principle of the dungeon; or rather of its three functions – to enclose, to deprive of light and to hide – it preserves only the first and eliminates the other two. Full lighting and the eye of a supervisor capture better than darkness, which ultimately protected. Visibility is a trap. (Foucault 1995, 200)

DOI: 10.1057/9781137476661.0008

This *panopticon* is also an image of our modern society, Foucault argued. Our government watches us, and in general, we don't commit crimes because we know we could be caught. It is important that we know that we might be watched at any time, but that we can never know for sure whether we are watched now. 'Power should be visible and unverifiable,' Foucault wrote, 'the inmate must never know whether he is being looked at at any one moment, but he must be sure that he may always be so' (201). George Orwell's novel *Nineteen Eighty-Four* (1949) describes this kind of intensely surveilled state perfectly.

In the decades since Foucault wrote about the panopticon, the nature of surveillance has changed greatly. We are watched to a far greater degree than when Foucault was alive, with surveillance cameras on every street corner and the NSA and many other entities able to access our emails or phone calls. It's not clear that today's surveillance functions in the regulatory way Foucault described, disciplining us to be well-behaved citizens. Surveillance has become complicated in the digital age. Even the word has been altered. Roger Clarke defined dataveillance (1988) as 'the systematic monitoring of people's actions or communications through the application of information technology'. Steve Mann and collaborators coined other variations. Sousveillance plays upon the French word *sous,* meaning 'under', in contrast to *sur* which means 'over', and it refers to ordinary citizens watching authorities, for instance using wearable cameras. Coveillance is peers watching each other (Mann, Nolan, and Wellman 2003).

In his book *The Googlization of Everything*, Siva Vaidhyanathan argues that we need a new term to describe today's surveillance, as it is fundamentally different from the panopticon Foucault described. Vaidhyanathan proposes the term *cryptopticon*. The most important thing about today's cryptopticon, Vaidhyanathan (2011) writes, is that 'we don't know all the ways in which we are being watched or profiled – we simply know that we are. And we don't regulate our behavior under the gaze of surveillance. Instead, we don't seem to care' (112). According to Vaidhyanathan, we don't know all the ways in which we are being watched, but we know that they are extensive, and that we are watched by many different entities: governments, corporations and criminals.

In the years after Vaidhyanathan coined the term cryptopticon we have debated the Snowden leaks and had ongoing discussions of how Facebook and other web services track us, and we actually know quite a lot more about how we are being watched. In many cases we know exactly

DOI: 10.1057/9781137476661.0008

how we are being watched. For instance, several companies are now offering discounts on health insurance to employees who agree to wear a Fitbit activity tracker (Olson and Tilley 2014, Olson 2014). Progressive, a US car insurance company, offers its customers a device they call the Snapshot that will track their driving for 30 days, and promise a discount to drivers the Snapshot device finds drive less than average, in safer ways and at safer times of the day (Huffman 2013; Progressive 2014). Wild-flower Health is a company that offers a pregnancy tracker, Due Date Plus, that is marketed to insurance companies and large employers. Due Date Plus is already offered to all women in Wyoming who are covered by Medicaid, and it seems very similar to many other pregnancy tracking apps available, letting you track weight and other measurements. There are some added benefits for users such as access to calling a nurse at any time of the day or night, but most importantly for the health care provider, the app 'uses self-reported data to identify high-risk pregnan-cies and drive interventions' (DeGheest 2013). Maternity and newborn care are a major expense in health care, so if high-risk pregnancies can be caught early on, better care can be provided and a lot of money, and possibly lives, can be saved.

As Mae thinks in *The Circle*, 'what had always caused her anxiety, or stress, or worry, was not any one force, nothing independent and exter-nal – it wasn't danger to herself or the constant calamity of other people and their problems. It was internal: it was subjective, it was *not knowing*' (Eggers 2013, 194).

The fantasy of absolute self-knowledge through technology, backed up with the knowledge that the software will call in experts (doctors, nurses, hospitals) is very seductive. If my data shows me (and my insurer) that I am a safe driver, that I am doing a great job looking after my baby, or that I am walking 10,000 steps a day and doing my best to stay healthy, I will feel good about myself. If I can look at graphs showing that my weight gain during pregnancy is normal and that the baby is growing well I'll feel safe. I might feel differently if I wasn't able to keep up the 10,000 steps my employer required or if I started admitting to my pregnancy tracker that I wasn't getting enough sleep or was eating nothing but ice cream.

These apps are only the beginning. The technology is here, and we are just starting to find ways to use it. Remember the smart onesies and baby monitors I wrote about in the last chapter? Imagine if Wyoming Medic-aid starts offering smart onesies to newborns that track breathing, sleep, heart rate, temperature, feeding and more. Imagine if you start getting visits from child services if your baby doesn't get enough sleep or there are other risk indicators. That might also save lives, but imagine parenting under constant government surveillance. These transactions – our data for a discount or for health care – will quite likely save lives, but it is very easy to see how they can be abused. And this technology is already here.

Seeing ourselves

When we willingly share data from an activity tracker, a safe driving monitor or a health app with our employer or insurer, we willingly trade our personal data in return for lower costs or better services. Sometimes we might appreciate being 'seen,' whether we feel that we are seen by the technology or by our health care providers or insurers. But, importantly, these apps allow us to see ourselves. As I discussed in chapter 5, studies have found that people develop 'affective ties' to the data they track (Oxlund 2012, 50; Ruckenstein 2014; Rooksby et al. 2014), just as our diaries, blogs, selfies and family photo albums are meaningful to us.

Apps which allow us to see our own data allow us to see ourselves. We look at our data doubles as we gazed into the mirror as teenagers wondering who we were and who we might be. We look at our data in much the same ways as you might flick through your selfies to find the one that shows you the way you want to be seen.

When Parmigianino painted his *Self-Portrait in a Convex Mirror* in 1524, he painted himself exactly as he saw himself, using the best technology available to him. His image is distorted due to the convex shape of the mirror he used. Our self-representations are always distorted in some way. The data doubles that are generated by our health trackers or productivity apps are not complete or even entirely accurate likenesses any more than Parmigianino's self-portrait was, although it may be harder for us to see how they are distorted.

Parmigianino's self-portrait hangs in an art gallery nearly half a millennium after he painted it. Millions of people must have seen his self-portrait or a photograph of it over the years. But unlike our contemporary self-representations, it was not analysed by data brokers, search engines, marketers and governments. The audience for our self-representations is no longer, as a few decades ago, ourselves and each other. Our audience today includes machines. The machines parse the

DOI: 10.1057/9781137476661.0008

data we provide, running selfies through facial recognition software, our status updates through sentiment analysis software, our health data through risk indication analyses, and send the results on to marketers, employers, insurers or governments. Machines helped us create those self-representations in the first place.

And yet, we continue to express ourselves. We are humans, after all. 'Photography is power,' Susan Sontag wrote (1973, 8). Selfies and other self-representations can be seen as a way of taking back this power, just as UPS drivers track their supervisors and protestors turn cameras on the police.

In practice, for now, we don't think too much about our machine audiences. We are too busy learning more about ourselves and each other by taking selfies, writing blogs, talking together on Facebook or Tumblr. We no longer need to rely on others to represent us. We represent ourselves.

DOI: 10.1057/9781137476661.0008

References

Alper, Meryl. 2013. 'War on Instagram: Framing Conflict Photojournalism with Mobile Photography Apps.' *New Media & Society,* September, 1461444813504265. doi:10.1177/1461444813504265.

Angwin, Julia. 2014. *Dragnet Nation: A Quest for Privacy, Security, and Freedom in a World of Relentless Surveillance.* New York: Times Books.

Arthur, Charles. 2011. 'iPhone Keeps Record of Everywhere You Go.' *The Guardian.* 20 April. http://www.theguardian.com/technology/2011/apr/20/iphone-tracking-prompts-privacy-fears.

Baden, Karl. 2007. *Every Day: Confusing Art and Obsession since 1987.* Blog documenting art project. http://kbeveryday.blogspot.com.

Barker, Roger G. (ed.) 1963. *The Stream of Behavior: Explorations of Its Structure and Content.* East Norwalk, CT, US: Appleton-Century-Crofts. http://psycnet.apa.org/books/11177/.

Barker, Roger G., and Herbert F. Wright. 1951. *One Boy's Day: A Specimen Record of Behavior.* Oxford: Harper.

Barthes, Roland. 1981. *Camera Lucida: Reflections on Photography.* New York: Hill and Wang.

Beadle, John. 1656. *The Journal or Diary of a Thankful Christian: Presented in Some Meditations upon Numb. 33.2.* London: E. Cotes for Tho. Parkhurst. https://archive.org/details/journaloroobead.

Boesel, Whitney Erin. 2013. 'Track Me, Baby.' *Cyborgology.* 8 August. http://thesocietypages.org/cyborgology/2013/08/08/track-me-baby/.

Bogost, Ian. 2007. *Persuasive Games: The Expressive Power of Videogames*. Cambridge, MA: MIT Press.

Borzello, Frances. 1998. *Seeing Ourselves: Women's Self-Portraits*. New York: Harry N. Abrams.

Bosker, Bianca. 2014. 'Nice to Meet You. I've Already Taken Your Picture.' *Huffington Post*. 10 February. http://www.huffingtonpost.com/2014/02/10/narrative-clip_n_4760580.html.

Bourdieu, Pierre. 1990. *Photography: A Middle-Brow Art*. Stanford: Stanford University Press.

boyd, danah. 2014. *It's Complicated: The Social Lives of Networked Teens*. New Haven: Yale University Press.

Breton, André. 1969. *Manifestoes of Surrealism*. Ann Arbor: University of Michigan Press.

Bridle, James. 2011. 'Where the F**k Was I? (A Book).' *BookTwo.org*. http://booktwo.org/notebook/where-the-f-k-was-i/.

———. 2014. 'The New Aesthetic.' Blog post at *Really Interesting Group*. 6 May. http://www.riglondon.com/blog/2011/05/06/the-new-aesthetic/.

British Airways. 2014. *The Happiness Blanket*. YouTube, 29 June. https://www.youtube.com/watch?v=90F0-28MOoU.

Brown, Rebecca (Beckieo). 2014. 'Photo Every Day. 6 1/2 Years.' *YouTube*. 8 June. https://www.youtube.com/watch?annotation_id=annotation_788633&feature=iv&src_vid=ACU7xpM4s6Q&v=eRvk5UQY1Js.

Bucher, Taina. 2012. 'Want to Be on the Top? Algorithmic Power and the Threat of Invisibility on Facebook.' *New Media and Society* 14 (7, 1 November): 1164–80. doi:10.1177/1461444812440159.

Burke, Kenneth. 1968. *Language as Symbolic Action: Essays on Life, Literature, and Method*. Berkeley: University of California Press.

Burns, Anne. 2013– (ongoing). *The Carceral Net: Photography, Feminism and Social Media's Disciplinary Principle*. Research blog. http://thecarceralnet.wordpress.com.

Chartier, Roger. 2001. 'The Practical Impact of Writing.' In *The Book History Reader*, edited by David Finkelstein and Alistair McCleery. London: Routledge.

Chronos. 2014. Chronos – Find Your Time. http://getchronos.com Accessed 28 May 2014.

Chun, Wendy Hui Kyong. 2011. *Programmed Visions: Software and Memory*. Cambridge, MA: MIT Press.

Clarke, Roger. 1988. 'Information Technology and Dataveillance.' *Communications of the ACM* 31 (5): 498–512.

DOI: 10.1057/9781137476661.0009

Couser, G. Thomas. 2012. *Memoir: An Introduction*. New York: Oxford University Press.

Cramer, Henriette, Mattias Rost, and Lars Erik Holmquist. 2011. 'Performing a Check-in: Emerging Practices, Norms and "Conflicts" in Location-Sharing Using Foursquare.' In *Proceedings of the 13th International Conference on Human Computer Interaction with Mobile Devices and Services*, 57–66. MobileHCI '11. New York: ACM. doi:10.1145/2037373.2037384. http://doi.acm.org/10.1145/2037373.2037384.

Dean, Jodi. 2010. *Blog Theory: Feedback and Capture in the Circuits of Drive*. Cambridge, UK: Polity Press.

DeGheest, Anne. 2013. 'HealthTech Capital Invests in WildFlower Health.' *HealthTech Capital Blog*, 11 December. http://www.healthtechcapital.com/blog/anne_degheest/healthtech_capital_invests_in_wildflower_health/.

Van Dijck, José. 2007. *Mediated Memories in the Digital Age*. Stanford, CA: Stanford UP.

Van Dijck, José. 2014. 'Datafication, Dataism and Dataveillance: Big Data between Scientific Paradigm and Ideology.' *Surveillance & Society* 12 (2): 197–208.

Dmitrow-Devold, Karolina. 2013. ' "Superficial! Body Obsessed! Commercial!" Norwegian Press Representations of Girl Bloggers.' *Girlhood Studies* 6 (2): 65–82.

Drucker, Johanna. 2011. 'Humanities Approaches to Graphical Display.' *Digital Humanities Quarterly* 5 (1). http://www.digitalhumanities.org/dhq/vol/5/1/000091/000091.html.

Eggers, Dave. 2013. *The Circle*. New York: Alfred A. Knopf.

Elliott, Chris. 2014. 'Why an Article on Lisa Bonchek Adams Was Removed from the Guardian Site.' *The Guardian*, 16 January, sec. Comment is free. http://www.theguardian.com/commentisfree/2014/jan/16/why-article-lisa-bonchek-adams-removed.

Enli, Gunn Sara, and Nancy Thumim. 2012. 'Socializing and Self-Representation Online: Exploring Facebook.' *Observatorio (OBS*)* 6 (1). http://obs.obercom.pt/index.php/obs/article/view/489.

Foucault, Michel. 1988. *Technologies of the Self: A Seminar with Michel Foucault*. Eds. Luther H. Martin, Huck Gutman, and Patrick. H. Hutton. Cambridge, MA: University of Massachusetts Press.

DOI: 10.1057/9781137476661.0009

——. 1995. *Discipline and Punish: The Birth of the Prison.* New York: Random House.

Frank, Priscilla. 2012. 'Behind the Curtain: The Aesthetics of Photobooth at Musee De L'Elysee' *Huffington Post.* 17 March. http://www.huffingtonpost.com/2012/03/17/behind-the-curtain_n_1296434.html.

Franklin, Benjamin. 2007. *The Autobiography of Benjamin Franklin.* Orig. pub. 1791. New York: Cosimo.

Friday. 2014. Friday: Automated Journal. Google Play. https://play.google.com/store/apps/details?id=com.dexetra.friday&hl=en Accessed 3 April 2014.

Garber, Megan. 'On Live-Tweeting One's Suffering.' *The Atlantic,* 13 January 2014. http://www.theatlantic.com/technology/archive/2014/01/on-live-tweeting-ones-suffering/283013/.

Gates, Kelly. 2011. *Our Biometric Future.* New York: New York University Press.

Gillespie, Tarleton. 2014. 'Facebook's Algorithm – Why Our Assumptions Are Wrong, and Our Concerns Are Right.' Blog post to *Culture Digitally: Examining Contemporary Cultural Production,* 4 July. http://culturedigitally.org/2014/07/facebooks-algorithm-why-our-assumptions-are-wrong-and-our-concerns-are-right/.

Glas, René. 2011. 'Breaking Reality: Exploring Pervasive Cheating in Foursquare.' In *Proceedings of DIGRA.* http://www.digra.org/wp-content/uploads/digital-library/11307.57380.pdf.

Goffman, Erving. 1959. *The Presentation of Self in Everyday Life.* New York: Anchor.

Greco, Diane. 2004. 'Body by Blogger.' Blog post, 25 February. *Narcissism, Vanity, Exhibitionism, Ambition, Vanity, Vanity, Vanity,* https://web.archive.org/web/20040407142959/http://home.earthlink.net/~dianegreco/oldwhinges.html.

Gregg, Melissa. 2014. 'Counterproductive: Towards Mindful Labor.' *Home Cooked Theory.* 3 March. http://homecookedtheory.com/archives/2014/03/13/counterproductive-towards-mindful-labor/.

Haggerty, Kevin D., and Richard V. Ericson. 2000. 'The Surveillant Assemblage.' *The British Journal of Sociology* 51 (4): 605–22. doi:10.1080/00071310020015280.

Hall, James. 2014. *The Self-Portrait: A Cultural History.* New York: Themes and Hudson. Kindle edition.

Hayles, N. Katherine. 2004. 'Print Is Flat, Code Is Deep: Rethinking Signification in New Media.' *Poetics Today* 25 (1): 67–90.

DOI: 10.1057/9781137476661.0009

Heehs, Peter. 2013. *Writing the Self: Diaries, Memoirs, and the History of the Self*. New York: Bloomsbury.

Hill, Kashmir. 2012. 'How Target Figured out a Teen Girl Was Pregnant before Her Father Did.' *Forbes.com*, 16 February. http://www.forbes.com/sites/kashmirhill/2012/02/16/how-target-figured-out-a-teen-girl-was-pregnant-before-her-father-did/.

Hooper, Clare, and Jill Walker Rettberg. 2011. 'Experiences with Geographical Collaborative Systems: Playfulness in Geosocial Networks and Geocaching.' In Stockholm, Sweden. http://eprints.soton.ac.uk/272471/1/MobileHCI_workshop_CJH.pdf.

Huffman, Mark. 2013. 'What You Should Know Before Trying Progressive's Snapshot.' *Consumer Affairs*. 27 June. http://www.consumeraffairs.com/news/what-you-should-know-before-trying-progressives-snapshot-062713.html.

Iser, Wolfgang. 2014. 'The Reading Process: A Phenomenological Approach.' In *Modern Criticism and Theory: A Reader*, edited by David Lodge and Nigel Wood, 3rd edn. London: Longman, 294–310.

Ivonin, Leonid, Huang-Ming Chang, Wei Chen, and Matthias Rauterberg. 2012. 'Unconscious Emotions: Quantifying and Logging Something We Are Not Aware of.' *Personal and Ubiquitous Computing* 17 (4, April): 663–73.

Jacob, Kurdin. 2013. *'Facebook Is My Second Home'. The Kurdish Diaspora's Use of Facebook in Shaping a Nation*. MA thesis, University of Bergen. http://hdl.handle.net/1956/7629.

Kalina, Noah. 2006. 'Everyday.' *YouTube*. 26 August. https://www.youtube.com/watch?v=6B26asyGKDo.

Keller, Bill. 2014. 'Heroic Measures.' *The New York Times*, 12 January. http://www.nytimes.com/2014/01/13/opinion/keller-heroic-measures.html.

Keller, Emma. 2014. 'Forget Funeral Selfies. What Are the Ethics of Tweeting a Terminal Illness?' *The Guardian*, 8 January, sec. Comment is free. http://www.theguardian.com/commentisfree/2014/jan/08/lisa-adams-tweeting-cancer-ethics.

Kirschenbaum, Matthew. 2012. *Mechanisms: New Media and the Forensic Imagination*. Cambridge, MA: MIT Press.

Kramer, Adam D. I., Guillory, Jamie E., and Hancock, Jeffrey T. 2014. 'Experimental Evidence of Massive-Scale Emotional Contagion through Social Networks.' *PNAS* 111 (24): 8788–90. doi:10.1073/pnas.1320040111.

DOI: 10.1057/9781137476661.0009

Leaver, Tama, and Tim Highfield. 2014. 'Mapping the Ends of Identity on Instagram.' Presentation given at the Australia and New Zealand Communications Association conference (ANZCA), 9–11 July, Melbourne. http://www.slideshare.net/Tama/mapping-the-ends-of-identity-on-instagram.

Lee, Ahree. 2006. 'Me.' *YouTube*. Uploaded 11 August. https://www.youtube.com/watch?v=55YYaJIrmzo.

Lejeune, Phillippe. 2001. 'How Do Diaries End?' *Biography* 24: 99–112.

Liebling, Abbott Joseph. 1960. 'Do You Belong in Journalism?' *New Yorker*, 14 May: 105.

Lien, Sigrid. 2014. ' "Buying an Instrument Does Not Necessarily Make You a Musician": Studio Photography and the Digital Revolution.' In *Digital Snaps: The New Face of Photography*, 131–54. London: I.B. Tauris.

Lindqvist, Janne, Justin Cranshaw, Jason Wiese, Jason Hong, and John Zimmerman. 2011. 'I'm the Mayor of My House: Examining Why People Use Foursquare - a Social-Driven Location Sharing Application.' In *Proceedings of the SIGCHI Conference on Human Factors in Computing Systems*, 2409–18. CHI '11. New York: ACM. doi:10.1145/1978942.1979295.

Losh, Elizabeth. 2014. 'Beyond Biometrics: Feminist Media Theory Looks at Selfiecity.' *Selfiecity.net*. http://selfiecity.net/#theory.

Lövheim, Mia. 2011. 'Young Women's Blogs as Ethical Spaces.' *Information, Communication & Society* 14 (3): 338–54.

Mann, Steve, Jason Nolan, and Barry Wellman. 2003. 'Sousveillance: Inventing and Using Wearable Computing Devices for Data Collection in Surveillance Environments.' *Surveillance & Society* 1 (3): 331–55.

Marcengo, Alessandro and Amon Rapp. 2014. 'Visualization of Human Behavior Data: The Quantified Self.' In *Innovative Approaches of Data Visualization and Visual Analytics*, edited by L. H. Huang and W. Huang, 236–65. Hershey, PA: IGI Global.

Markham, Annette N. 1998. *Life Online: Researching Real Experience in Virtual Space*. Ethnographic Alternatives Book Series. Walnut Creek, CA: Altamira.

——. 2013a. 'Dramaturgy of Digital Experience.' In *The Drama of Social Life: A Dramaturgical Handbook*, edited by C. Edgley, 279–94. Farnham, Surrey: Ashgate Press.

——. 2013b. 'Undermining "Data": A Critical Examination of a Core Term in Scientific Inquiry.' *First Monday*, 7 October, 18 (10). http://uncommonculture.org/ojs/index.php/fm/article/view/4868/3749.

DOI: 10.1057/9781137476661.0009

Marwick, Alice. 2013. *Status Update: Celebrity, Publicity, and Branding in the Social Media Age*. New Haven: Yale University Press.

Mateas, Michael. 2005. 'Procedural Literacy: Educating the New Media Practitioner.' *On the Horizon* 13 (2): 101–11. doi:10.1108/10748120510608133.

McCosker, Anthony, and Rowan Wilken. 2014. 'Rethinking "Big Data" as Visual Knowledge: The Sublime and the Diagrammatic in Data Visualisation.' *Visual Studies* 29 (2): 155–64. doi:10.1080/1472586X.2014.887268.

McFadden, Syreeta. 2014. 'Teaching the Camera to See My Skin.' *BuzzFeed*. http://www.buzzfeed.com/syreetamcfadden/teaching-the-camera-to-see-my-skin.

Mendelson, Andrew L., and Zizi Papacharissi. 2011. 'Look at Us: Collective Narcissism in College Student Facebook Photo Galleries.' In *A Networked Self: Identity, Community, and Culture on Social Network Sites*, edited by Zizi Papacharissi. New York: Routledge, 251–274.

Miall, Nina. 2014. 'Tehching Hsieh: One Year Performance 1980–1981.' Video of curator Nina Miall presenting and discussing Hsieh's work, for an exhibition at Carriageworks, Sydney, 29 April—6 July 2014.

Miller, Nancy K. 1991. *Getting Personal: Feminist Occasions and Other Autobiographical Acts*. New York: Routledge.

Molina, J. Michelle. 2008. 'Technologies of the Self: The Letters of Eighteenth-Century Mexican Jesuit Spiritual Daughters.' *History of Religions* 47 (4): 282–303. doi:10.1086/589802.

Montaigne, Michel de. 1910. 'On Presumption.' In *Essays of Montaigne*, vol. 6 of 10. Trans. Charles Cotton, edited by William Carew Hazlett. New York: Edwin C. Hill. http://oll.libertyfund.org/titles/168.

Mortensen, Torill, and Jill Walker. 2002. 'Blogging Thoughts: Personal Publication as an Online Research Tool,' in *Researching ICTs in Context*, edited by Andrew Morrison. Oslo: InterMedia, University of Oslo. http://www.intermedia.uio.no/konferanser/skikt-02/docs/Researching_ICTs_in_context-Ch11-Mortensen-Walker.pdf.

Murray, Janet H. 1997. *Hamlet on the Holodeck: The Future of Narrative in Cyberspace*. Cambridge, MA: MIT Press.

Narrative Clip. Narrative Clip – A Wearable, Automatic Lifelogging Camera. http://getnarrative.com Accessed 28 May, 2014.

Olson, Parmy. 2014. 'Wearable Tech Is Plugging into Health Insurance' *Forbes.com*, 19 June. http://www.forbes.com/sites/parmyolson/2014/06/19/wearable-tech-health-insurance/.

DOI: 10.1057/9781137476661.0009

Olson, Parmy, and Aaron Tilley. 2014. 'The Quantified Other: Nest and Fitbit Chase a Lucrative Side Business.' *Forbes.com*, 5 May. http://www.forbes.com/sites/parmyolson/2014/04/17/the-quantified-other-nest-and-fitbit-chase-a-lucrative-side-business/.

Oppenheimer, Gerald. 2013. 'Medical Care of Infants in the United States: A Review of Recent Work.' In *History of Medicine*, edited by Rebecca Greene, 103–28. Florence, KY: Taylor and Francis.

OptimizeMe. 2014. OptimizeMe – Lifelogging and Quantified Self Tracking Improvement App. http://optimizeme-app.com Accessed 28 May 2014.

Orwell, George. 1949. *Nineteen Eighty-Four*. New York: Hartcourt & Brace.

Oxlund, Bjarke. 2012. 'Living by Numbers.' *Suomen Antropologi: Journal of the Finnish Anthropological Society* 37 (3): 42–56.

Palmgren, Ann-Charlotte. 2010. 'Posing My Identity. Today's Outfit in Swedish Blogs.' (*OBS**) *Observatorio* 4 (2). http://www.obs.obercom.pt/index.php/obs/article/viewArticle/294.

Pedercini, Paolo. 2014. 'Videogames and the Spirit of Capitalism.' *La Molleindustria*. http://www.molleindustria.org/blog/videogames-and-the-spirit-of-capitalism/.

Pellicer, Raynal. 2010. *Photobooth: The Art of the Automatic Portrait*. New York: Abrams.

Progressive. 2014. *Snapshot*. http://www.progressive.com/auto/snapshot/.

Reigeluth, Tyler Butler. 2014. 'Why Data Is Not Enough: Digital Traces as Control of Self and Self-Control.' *Surveillance & Society* 12 (2): 243–54.

Rettberg, Jill Walker. 2000–ongoing. jill/txt. Weblog. http://jilltxt.net
——. 2009. ' "Freshly Generated for You, and Barack Obama": How Social Media Represent Your Life.' *European Journal of Communication* 24 (4): 451–66. doi:10.1177/0267323109345715.
——. 2014. *Blogging*. 2nd ed. Cambridge: Polity Press.

Rettberg, Scott. 2008. 'Corporate Ideology in World of Warcraft.' In *Digital Culture, Play, and Identity: A World of Warcraft Reader*, edited by Hilde Corneliussen and Jill Walker Rettberg, 19–38. Cambridge, MA: MIT Press.

Rooksby, John, Mattias Rost, Alistair Morrison, and Matthew Chalmers. 2014. 'Personal Tracking as Lived Informatics.' In *Proceedings of the 32Nd Annual ACM Conference on Human Factors in Computing Systems,*

DOI: 10.1057/9781137476661.0009

1163–72. CHI '14. New York: ACM. doi:10.1145/2556288.2557039. http://doi.acm.org/10.1145/2556288.2557039.

Roth, Lorna. 2009. 'Looking at Shirley, the Ultimate Norm: Colour Balance, Image Technologies, and Cognitive Equity.' *Canadian Journal of Communication* 34 (1). http://www.cjc-online.ca/index.php/journal/article/view/2196.

Ruckenstein, Minna. 2014. 'Visualized and Interacted Life: Personal Analytics and Engagements with Data Doubles.' *Societies* 4 (1): 68–84. doi:10.3390/soc4010068.

Rutten, Ellen. 2014. '(Russian) Writer-Bloggers: Digital Perfection and the Aesthetics of Imperfection.' *Journal of Computer-Mediated Communication*, May, n/a–n/a. doi:10.1111/jcc4.12086.

Senft, Theresa M. 2008. *Camgirls: Celebrity and Community in the Age of Social Networks*. New York: Peter Lang.

——. 2013. 'Microcelebrity and the Branded Self.' In *A Companion to New Media Dynamics*, edited by John Hartley, Jean Burgess, and Axel Bruns, 347–55. Chicester: Wiley.

Serfaty, Viviane. 2004. *The Mirror and the Veil: An Overview of American Online Diaries and Blogs*. Amsterdam: Amsterdam Monographs in American Studies.

Shklovsky, Victor. 1988. 'Art as Technique.' In *Modern Criticism and Theory*, edited by David Lodge, 15–30. Original publication 1917. London: Longman.

Simanowski, Roberto. 2012. 'The Compelling Charm of Numbers: Writing For and Thru the Network of Data'. In *Remediating the Social*, edited by Simon Biggs. ELMCIP: Edinburgh. http://elmcip.net/critical-writing/compelling-charm-numbers-writing-and-thru-network-data.

Sontag, Susan. 1973. *On Photography*. New York: Picador.

Step. 2014. STEP Journal. http://www.step.pe Accessed 28 May 2014.

Stewart, Dodai. 2014. 'The Truth about Photography and Brown Skin.' *Jezebel*. 3 April. http://jezebel.com/the-truth-about-photography-and-brown-skin-1557656792.

Tietchen, Todd. 2014. 'Frank O'Hara and the Poetics of the Digital.' *Criticism* 56 (1): 45–61.

Tiidenberg, Katrin. 2014. 'Bringing Sexy Back: Reclaiming the Body Aesthetic via Self-Shooting.' *Cyberpsychology: Journal of Psychosocial Research on Cyberspace* 8 (1). doi:10.5817/CP2014-1-3. http://cyberpsychology.eu/view.php?cisloclanku=2014021701&article=3.

DOI: 10.1057/9781137476661.0009

Tompkins, Jane. 1989. 'Me and My Shadow.' In *Gender and Theory: Dialogues on Feminist Criticism*, edited by Linda Kauffman. New York: Basil Blackwell.

Uimonen, Paula. 2013. 'Visual Identity in Facebook.' *Visual Studies* 28 (2): 122–35. doi:10.1080/1472586X.2013.801634.

Vaidhyanathan, Siva. 2011. *The Googlization of Everything (and Why We Should Worry)*. Berkeley, CA: University of California Press.

Vertesi, Janet. 2014. 'My Experiment Opting Out of Big Data Made Me Look Like a Criminal.' *Time*, May. http://time.com/83200/privacy-internet-big-data-opt-out/.

Walker, Jill. 2003. *Fiction and Interaction: How Clicking a Mouse Can Make You Part of a Fictional World*. Dr. art. thesis, University of Bergen. http://www.ub.uib.no/elpub/2003/d/517001.

——. 2005a. 'Weblog.' In *The Routledge Encyclopedia of Narrative Theory*, edited by David Herman, Manfred Jahn, and Marie-Laure Ryan, 45. London and New York: Routledge.

——. 2005b. 'Mirrors and Shadows: The Digital Aestheticisation of Oneself'. In the proceedings of Digital Arts and Culture. 1–3 December 2005. Copenhagen: IT University of Copenhagen: 184–90. http://hdl.handle.net/1956/1136.

——. 2006. 'Blogging from Inside the Ivory Tower.' In *Uses of Blogs*, edited by Axel Bruns and Joanne Jacobs. New York: Peter Lang, 127–138.

Warfield, Katie. 2014. 'Why I Love Selfies and You Should Too (Damn It)' Public lecture at Kwantlen Polytechnic University, 26 March 2014. Published on *YouTube*, 2 April 2014. https://www.youtube.com/watch?v=aOVIJwy3nVo

Washburn, Dan. 2006. 'Her: The 1,000 faces of Ahree Lee.' *Shanghaiist*, 14 August. http://shanghaiist.com/2006/08/14/her_the_1000_fa.php.

Winner, Langdon. 1980. 'Do Artifacts Have Politics?' *Daedalus* 109 (1): 121–36.

Wyatt, Sally. 2007. 'Technological Determinism Is Dead; Long Live Technological Determinism.' In *Handbook of Science and Technology Studies*, edited by Edward J Hackett, Olga Amsterdamska, Michael E. Lynch and Judy Wajcman, 165–80, 3rd ed. Cambridge, MA: MIT Press.

DOI: 10.1057/9781137476661.0009

OPEN

Index

DOI: 10.1057/9781137476661.0009

Greco, Diane, 30
Gregg, Melissa, 74
growth chart, 66

happiness blankets, 73
Hayles, N. Katherine, 56, 57
Heyday, 58
Hsieh, Tehching, 95

Instagram, 21, 22, 25, 26, 29, 46, 52, 54
insurance companies and data
    collection, 83, 86
iPhone, 27, 46, 72, 78

Jawbone Up, 62
JenniCam, 51
Journals
    baby journal, 22

Kodak, 28

Lejeune, Philippe, 46, 57, 58
Lien, Sigrid, 54
lifelogging, 26, 47, 52, 60
    activity, 75
    calories, 74
    heart-rate variability, 69
    unconscious emotions, 73

machines as active cognizers, 56
Mann, Steve, 51, 52, 85
maps, 76
Markham, Annette, 22, 69, 95
Marwick, Alice, 23
McFadden, Syreeta, 29, 30
Mimo Baby, 67
Minutely, 71
mirror, 87
Misfit Shine, 62, 65, 70, 75
misrepresentation, 29
Murray, Janet, 59
MyFitnessPal, 74, 75

Narrative Clip, 26, 51, 52, 53, 54, 55, 56
Nest, 82
new aesthetic, 78

O'Hara, Frank, 98
OptimizeMe, 48
Orwell, George, 85
Oxlund, Bjarke, 71

panopticon, 85
Parmigianino, 28, 87
photo album, 24, 30
Plazes.com, 46
pregnancy, 66, 81
pregnancy tracker, 86
punctum, 55, 56, 63

Quantified Self, 63

Reddit, 23
Reigeluth, Tyler Butler, 69
Rettberg, Scott, 58
rhetoric of failure, 59
Rooksby, John, 58
Roth, Lorna, 28
Ruckenstein, Minna, 68, 69, 71
Runkeeper, 47, 57, 58, 62
Rutten, Ellen, 52, 98

Saga, 47, 48
school, 47, 52, 77, 83
selfies, viii, 26, 27, 28, 29, 30, 53, 80, 83
self improvement, 60
self-tracking, 46, 57, 62, 63
Senft, Theresa, viii, 51
Shirley cards, 28
Shklovsky, Victor, 26
Simanowski, Roberto, 31
SkinneePix, 27
skin tone bias, 29
sleep, 49, 62, 63, 64, 65, 66, 71, 75
Sontag, Susan, 25, 69, 80, 88
souveillance, 72
Spreadsheets, 72, 73
Sprout Baby, 23
studium, 55, 63
Swarm, 77

Target, 81
technological determinism, 28

DOI: 10.1057/9781137476661.0009